WESTRAY

WESTRAY

My Journey from Darkness to Light

VERNON THERIAULT *as told to* **MARJORIE COADY**
Foreword by **STEVE HUNT**, *United Steelworkers*

Nimbus Publishing Limited
3660 Strawberry Hill Street, Halifax, NS, B3K 5A9
(902) 455-4286 nimbus.ca

Printed and bound in Canada

NB1356

Design: Jenn Embree

Library and Archives Canada Cataloguing in Publication
    Theriault, Vernon, 1961-, author
    Westray : my journey from darkness to light / Vernon Theriault as
    told to Marjorie Coady ; preface from Steve Hunt, United Steelworkers.
    Issued in print and electronic formats.
    ISBN 978-1-77108-674-5 (softcover).—ISBN 978-1-77108-675-2 (HTML)

1. Theriault, Vernon, 1961-. 2. Coal miners—Nova Scotia—Plymouth
(Pictou)—Biography. 3. Coal mine accidents—Nova Scotia—Plymouth
(Pictou). 4. Westray Mine Disaster, Plymouth, Pictou, N.S., 1992. 5. Post-
traumatic stress disorder. 6. Autobiographies. I. Coady, Majorie, author
II. Title.

HD8039.M62C3 2018   331.7'622334092   C2018-902933-1
                                                     C2018-902934-X

Nimbus Publishing acknowledges the financial support for its publishing activities
from the Government of Canada through the Canada Book Fund (CBF) and
the Canada Council for the Arts, and from the Province of Nova Scotia. We are
pleased to work in partnership with the Province of Nova Scotia to develop and
promote our creative industries for the benefit of all Nova Scotians.

To my wife, Marilyn,

and my children,

Aaron, James, and Lindsey,

for their constant love and support

during this journey

—☙—

"The consensus of the experts suggests strongly that Westray was an accident waiting to happen."

— *The Westray Story: A Predictable Path to Disaster*, Report of the Westray Mine Public Inquiry, Justice K. Peter Richard

CONTENTS

Labour activists and family members march in New Glasgow, demanding that the tragedy of Westray not be repeated. The author is in the second row, third from the left.

FOREWORD

ON MAY 9, 1992, AN UNDERGROUND METHANE EXPLOSION RIPPED through the Westray coal mine in Plymouth, Nova Scotia, killing twenty-six miners and forever changing the communities of Pictou County. In the time that followed, the public came to learn that the disaster was caused by a reckless disregard for miners' safety, poor oversight by government regulators, and mismanagement of the mine. It was, and remains, the blackest of marks on Canadian history.

Out of this tragedy emerged a determination that there would be "No More Westrays." The United Steelworkers stood shoulder to shoulder with the Westray families and the surrounding communities, to demand justice and to undertake a lobbying campaign of federal politicians for tougher laws that would hold corporations criminally accountable where their negligence results in the death of a worker.

Vernon Theriault was a leading figure in that fight for justice, and he hasn't stopped fighting. Vernon was a Westray miner who had been at the mine twelve hours before the explosion and then worked on the rescue and recovery team. His courageous actions that day earned him a Medal of Bravery from the governor general. But the real heroism of Vernon's story comes after.

Vernon worked with the United Steelworkers for years of intense lobbying to pass the "Westray Law." At a time when it would have been understandable for Vernon to step back, he stepped forward. He told us that he could not read or write. We asked him to tell his story and he has. Vernon's fight did not end at the mine, and the story he tells should inspire all of us to fight even if we think we have limitations. The prime minister called Vernon and others heroes, and then the system tried to leave them all behind. He understood that the only way to honour the memories of his fallen co-workers was to fight for change, to make sure nothing like Westray ever happened again. Because of Vernon's commitment, determination, and willingness to fight, Members of Parliament unanimously passed the "Westray Law" in late 2003. It remains a significant achievement for working people. Today, our fight to have the law enforced continues and Vernon continues to be there with us every step of the way.

— **Steve Hunt,**
United Steelworkers,
western Canadian director

PREFACE

THIS STORY IS ABOUT MUCH MORE THAN WESTRAY.

I was raised in Pictou County but moved to Halifax in my early twenties because of the bleak work prospects within the area.

Having given birth to my twin boys the month before the Westray explosion, I knew little about the tragedy. Although my grandfather—Vernon's grandfather and mine were brothers—was a miner at the Drummond mine located in Westville, I knew little to nothing about mining. Busy being a first-time mom, I remember hearing about the explosion at Plymouth, and that my cousin Vernon had narrowly missed being one of the miners caught underground. I didn't know Vernon as well as I knew his sister Nancy (we worked together at the New Glasgow McDonald's in the late '70s/early '80s).

I moved back home from Halifax in 2003, and retired from Bell Aliant in 2010 after twenty-three years' service in various departments. In late 2013, I met Nancy and Vernon at a grocery store in New Glasgow. As we were catching up with each others' lives, the conversation turned to Vernon who said that he wanted to write a book about his Westray experience. Having twenty years' (pre-press) experience in the printing industry, a flair for words, and at loose ends, I agreed to help him with his memoirs.

Working together at his kitchen table over the next several years, my eyes were opened wide. Not only did Vernon survive Westray, he also had several hurdles to jump in his dealings with the Workers' Compensation Board. He lobbied for Bill C-45, known as The Westray Bill, and he struggled with illiteracy, which is more prevalent today than most people realize.

My hope is that the reader of this book enjoys and gains some knowledge from its contents. I feel this is a legacy to the next generation, and that if it helps even one person then the time (and emotion) it took to write is worthwhile.

— **Marjorie Coady,**
New Glasgow

INTRODUCTION

MAY 9, 1992, WAS A TRAGIC DAY IN PICTOU COUNTY HISTORY AND THE beginning of a long and life-changing journey for me.

It's been over two decades since the Westray mine disaster. After a series of bittersweet ceremonies commemorating the tragedy of twenty-five years ago in my community, I can't help but remember the events that put me here today, the sacrifices that I made along the way, and the knowledge I've gained.

In sharing my story my hope is that in some small way I can help anyone who is struggling with the issues that I encountered during my journey. Although the Westray disaster is predominant, it also opened the door to other issues that I feel are important as well.

I struggled with post-traumatic stress disorder after Westray. I discovered, when I was trying to retrain for alternate work, that I was dyslexic, which in turn caused my illiteracy. I also underwent numerous surgeries (of which two were on my back).

I found a new purpose when I became involved in the labour lobby to bring in a federal bill to protect worker safety. I am honoured to be writing this book because I am the only person to have worked in the Westray mine, to have taken part in the rescue, *and* to have been part of the campaign to make Bill C-45, known as the Westray Bill, law.

— Vernon Theriault,
New Glasgow

PART ONE

IN THE
MINE

CHAPTER 1

A GOOD JOB WITH GOOD PAY

"The Westray mine is located at Plymouth, near Stellarton, in Pictou County, Nova Scotia. Westray was the only operating underground coal mine in Pictou County at the time of the explosion. The Pictou coalfield had been mined for some 200 years, and elements of the disaster rest in the nature of that coalfield with its thick and gassy seams. The Foord seam, which Westray was mining, has hosted at least eight mines."
—THE WESTRAY REPORT

APRIL 1987

I WAS EMPLOYED AT GOOD-WEAR TIRE SHOP LOCATED ON STELLARTON Road in New Glasgow. Jim Livingstone was the manager of the shop and had asked me to join their team. Two years previously I had worked with Jim at Andy's Tire Shop located on the Westville Road, also in New Glasgow. I enjoyed my time working with him; he was an excellent man to work for and with.

While employed at Good-Wear tire, we landed a contract with Westray Coal-Curragh Resources Inc. to supply, repair, and refurbish their tire needs. I can still recall to this day my first time arriving at the mine site. The company was just at the beginning of production and there were only two trailers on-site—one for employees and the other for equipment.

I was instructed to pick up several tires for repair. The road was not fully developed; there was no pavement in sight. It was like taking a camping road through the woods on a non-marked path. The site eventually improved with the addition of a building and the road was better grated. It was paved several years later.

Roman Schule (whose job title was master mechanic) was who I reported to in regards to their tire needs. Our contract was such that I was on call 24/7 and would be able to respond within minutes. Not long after I started going to the mine site on behalf of Good-Wear, I was called in to repair a tire on one of their machines. The machine was located down the tunnel of the Westray mine, but thankfully not too far down.

With my repair kit and tools in hand, I walked down the tunnel and repaired the tire. It was a weird experience—repairing the tire with water dripping on and around me like it was raining out. Roman was a stickler for being punctual; if the agreement was nine, then you were there at nine and not a minute after. I take pride in being dependable both at work and at home. Unfortunately, I would be challenged on this trait.

June 1990

On this particular day, four new tires were purchased for one of Westray's scoop loaders. My co-worker and I were in charge of shipping and receiving tires in the shop. With Westray's order in hand, we worked on the tires all day putting them together and filling them with calcium chloride, finally finishing all four tires in the early evening.

I suggested to my co-worker that we should load the tires on the delivery truck so they would be the first delivery of the day. After a long day, he wanted to load first thing in the morning as it was getting late and he had plans for the evening, which didn't include loading tires on a delivery truck.

Bright and early the next morning we loaded the delivery truck and headed over to the Westray mine site. When we arrived, we pulled up to the garage. We didn't even have a chance to get out of the truck when Roman stomped over. He was furious.

He informed us that since we were so late that he would not accept delivery. I proceeded to walk back to the truck and waited patiently while my co-worker tried to smooth over the ruffled feathers of our irate customer. After what seemed like a long time, with no visible results, my co-worker returned to the delivery truck.

My co-worker was discouraged, so I asked if I could try to persuade the customer to accept delivery. I'm an easygoing, soft-spoken guy, so when I approached the irate customer, he was receptive to my suggestions. Simply put, I gave him my personal guarantee that a situation such as this would not happen again. We were experiencing growing pains, I said, and I would personally take care of his account.

Any questions, concerns, orders, etc., speak with me directly, I told him—I'm your "go-to" guy. After giving Roman my personal guarantee, he accepted delivery of the tires he had ordered. From that day on, we became friends, and all his orders were directed to me. Whenever he called, I was there when I said I would be, sometimes a little early. I'm heavily involved in hockey, both playing and coaching. On one particular night, I was playing hockey in Stellarton when I got a call from the mine. Being a man of my word, I took off my gear, grabbed my keys, and headed out to the Westray mine to repair a tire.

December 1990

We were having our annual Christmas party at the tire shop. It was an informal affair and drop-ins were welcome. A former employee, John Munroe, had joined the gathering, and because it was informal

The author driving the Good-Wear truck in a Westville, Nova Scotia, Canada Day parade in 1990.

he brought along his brother, George. At the time, George happened to be employed at Westray. Because Westray was a major customer of ours, and I was the "go-to" guy, the conversation turned toward the mine. I informed George that I was a trained welder and was interested in obtaining employment at the mine as a welder. As the discussion progressed, he tried to discourage me from this endeavour.

November 1991

An employment opportunity arose at Westray for a welder. In 1980, I had trained as a welder in Sydney, Nova Scotia. When I took the Sydney course, I was lucky enough to have relatives who resided in Cape Breton (close to where my course was being held). Therefore, I could go to school during the week and return home to my wife and kids on the weekends. When I was younger, I can remember my grandmother saying, "get a trade so you'll always have something to fall back on." So, on her advice, I pursued a trade and the chance of a better-paying job.

In March 1983, I had the opportunity to upgrade my welding skills (high-pressure welding ticket) closer to home in Pictou County. The second course was held at the Pictou Regional Vocational School, since renamed the Nova Scotia Community College, Pictou Campus, located in Stellarton.

Despite my training, it was hard to find long-term welding work. I did manage to secure work twice at the Trenton car works, which manufactured steel railcars and underwent several name and owner changes over the years before finally closing its doors as a railcar manufacturer in 2007. When I worked there, it was owned by Hawker Siddeley. I was laid off twice and in the interim worked as a gas-station attendant to support my family. I eventually found employment at the tire shop, where wages were slightly higher.

Now in 1991, the job I yearned for had become available. During a routine delivery, Roman and I discussed a job opening. He was interested in my qualifications and wanted to see a sample of my welding skills. We arranged for me to return the following day to demonstrate my skills as a welder.

When I returned the next day, I performed the tasks he requested. When he inspected my work, he was impressed with my skill, informed me that it met with the requirements of the job opening, and that he would let me know of his decision shortly. When the call came at the shop later that day, I was told the opening was filled. Nepotism was in full force—one of the mine managers had hired his brother-in-law.

My disappointment was so transparent that Roman took pity on me and asked me to come see him at the mine site the next day. When I arrived at the site the next day, Roman escorted me to his office. Not knowing what was coming next, I waited for him to tell me what this impromptu meeting was about. He started with saying that there was twenty years' worth of work and the money was good.

The meeting then turned into a job interview when I was asked if I would be interested in becoming a coal miner. Roman was aware that I had a strong work ethic and would work as many hours as the company would give me. I was told that the wages could be up to sixty thousand dollars a year for someone who was willing to work. I was interested in the job but was unsure if I could work underground.

I had been married for eleven years, and by then Marilyn (nee Lennon) and I had three children: Aaron, born in 1981, James, born in 1984, and Lindsey, born in 1987. The oldest of five children, I was born in Sydney Mines, Cape Breton, in 1961.

While considering Roman's proposal, I shared with him my grandfather Roy Oliver's story of working in the mines both before and after the Second World War. Gramps worked in three of the mines in Nova Scotia, including Sydney Mines, Springhill, and Westville.

Although I was very young, I can still remember staying at my grandparents' house one summer in Sydney Mines. Early in the morning, we would meet at the table for breakfast. Gramps had a pet budgie, and the same routine was performed every morning. Gramps would open the cage and the bird would fly down on his plate and eat breakfast with us. We would talk about what the day had in store for us and share stories of what had happened the day before. These are among my fondest memories of my grandfather, and I cherish them to this day.

At the same time every morning, Gramps picked up his lunch box, put on his coat and hat, gave me a hug and kiss on the cheek, and headed out the door. Then Grandma and I would go back to bed for a few more hours of sleep. After sharing these memories with Roman, I asked if I could take a tour of the mine to see how it would affect me. *Maybe, since my grandfather worked underground in various mines, I could too; it just very well may be in the blood.*

The following day, I returned to the site with the intention of going underground. While nervously waiting for Roman, I was informed he was unavailable. An electrician who worked for the mine, a man named Brian Palmer, whom I knew casually because of my work in and around the mine, asked if I would like to accompany him down to the Number Ten Crossover.

Saying to myself, *this is my chance,* I agreed. Because of limited illumination and this being my first time underground in the mine, I had to have certain specialized equipment. There had to be a personal light source, so we went into a room to collect the equipment, including a hard hat with a battery-powered light attached (just like you see in the movies). Some work areas were dimly lit by machinery, but some had no machinery at all so the lighted hard hat was your only light source.

The transportation to take us underground was a transformed farm tractor. Because Brian worked in different areas and not for specified periods of time, his tractor was equipped to carry whatever tools he needed for the job at hand, and one to two passengers. The "crew" tractor had a permanently attached cart with built-in benches to seat eight to ten people.

We got on his tractor and headed down into the mine. We drove deeper and deeper until we arrived at an area where some men were working. While Brian was doing repairs to some equipment, I was chatting with the men who were there. When I informed them I was considering employment in their area of the mine, one guy said, "Are you crazy? Why would you want to work underground in a mine?" I thought to myself, *then why are you here?*

I told him about my conversation with Roman—twenty years' worth of work, good pay with benefits, unlimited overtime. If you're willing to work, which I was, the work was there. I had to return to the tire shop, and Brian couldn't return me to the surface because he wasn't finished with the job at hand. He gave me directions back to the Main tunnel, with instructions that I could wait there till someone came along to give me a drive to the top. Walking along with just my solitary lamplight for company, I wondered what I was getting myself into, and if I could do this for a living.

I patiently waited at the Main tunnel for thirty minutes and no vehicles came by going to the surface. Anxious to get back to Good-Wear before they sent a search party looking for me, I decided to return to the surface on my own. It took me a little over an hour, all the while not seeing a person or vehicle.

Because of my reputation for dependability, I was anxious to get back to work at the tire shop. I'd spent half the day at the mine site already. Upon my return to Good-Wear, I called Roman and accepted his job offer. After the call, I gave my employer two weeks' notice.

—*ᴄ∽*—

WORKING IN THE MINE

"The underground workers at Westray ranged from miners with more than 20 years of underground mining experience to new workers fresh out of school. About one-third of the Westray underground workers hired in 1992 had some previous coal mining experience, about one-third had previous underground experience in hard-rock mining, and about one-third had no prior underground work experience."
– THE WESTRAY REPORT

DECEMBER 1991

After I finished my two-weeks' notice at Good-Wear, I went to Westray and formally filled out an application even though I knew I had the job. In the employment application was a confidentiality agreement. In a nutshell, I couldn't discuss my job or anything about the mine off-site. I had no concerns about signing this agreement at the time.

Day two of orientation was safety training. There were three of us in total. One was a mechanic, the other was a general labourer, and then me, who was classified as a miner-in-training. The first part of orientation was a movie about open-pit mines, a form of surface mining, which I found confusing because Westray was an underground mine. When the movie was over, one of the managers demonstrated how to use a MSA W65 self-rescuer, which was like a respirator, and the proper way to put it over your mouth and nose.

WESTRAY COAL
A Division of Curragh Resources Inc.
HEALTH AND SAFETY POLICY

It is the policy of Westray Coal to promote and maintain a safe
and productive work environment for all employees.

An effective Health and Safety Program will provide protection for
you and the security of your family, the general public and the
Company. It must be emphasized that this Program is vital to our
future progress and growth.

The challenges of reducing hazards, risk control and health and
safety awareness can be met through consultation and cooperation
between all employees.

It is the personal responsibility of each member of the management
team to ensure:

The author's copy of the Westray health and safety policy.

To this day, I still don't know why the movie shown was about
an open-pit mine, not an underground mine. Didn't they have any
training films of underground? Surely, there must have been somewhere that had underground such as ours so that we could relate
to what we were seeing. After the demonstration, we were taken to
the locker room, assigned lockers, locks, a wrench, the self-rescuer,
and a hard hat capable of attaching a light to. Each individual was
responsible for purchasing his own belt to attach the work tools to.

After the locker room, we were then taken to what was called
the *dry area*. Here we were given a *hanger,* which looked like a steel
basket. In the basket you placed any equipment you used during
the shift including your boots, tools, and hard hat. The basket was
suspended from the ceiling on a hook, with additional hooks on the
sides for any work clothing you wore that day. The room temperature
was extremely warm and clothing became dry very quickly.

Each basket was equipped with a combination lock that only you
and the company had the combination to. After your first shift in the

mine, this basket was your primary locker; the one in the other room was for your street clothes. Your work clothes never left the mine site. All washing was done in-house; taking clothes home was not an option. The company took care of your work clothes from beginning to end.

Day three of orientation over, I was now on the job. I showed up for work, put on my work uniform, gathered my tools, and put on my lighted hard hat (this is all done in the dry area before every shift). Ready for work, I walked out to the waiting area with the other men. I attached the battery to my belt and put the light on my hard hat. I was ready to head underground.

We got on a tractor and drove to the area of the mine where we were assigned to work that day. For an inexperienced miner, there were two crews to which they were assigned in order to orient them to working underground. In the beginning, it was only eight-hour shifts, which, over time, increased to twelve hours. During the orientation period new employees were not eligible for overtime.

One crew was responsible for the belts, which transported the coal from underground all the way up to the surface. The main priority was keeping the belts running and free from debris. This job required a lot of walking because there were multiple belts that stretched for large spaces throughout the mine. The other crew, which I became a member of, was responsible for the arches (braces for the roof of the mine).

First on the agenda was to place arches for support of the roof in that area of the mine. The arches were huge—the size of an overpass (one lane) that you would typically drive under. Engineers determined where and how many arches would be placed in each area.

Each arch was made of solid steel—there were three pieces in total, and erected on-site. The straight sides had identical indentations in the sides (like a ladder) to put in additional braces for extra support with a steel plate welded on top. The top arch was one solid piece of steel, with plates welded on the bottom. When the sides were matched up, the two plates came together. The plates were then bolted together to make one structure.

For safety reasons, all the welding was supposed to be done above ground. A garage with all the necessary equipment to weld the plates onto the arches was located on-site. Supplies pertaining to the mine were readily available, if not on-site, then just a phone call away.

Behind the arches, galvanized aluminium forms (known to the workers as plates) were placed. To brace the plates we used lumber blocks of wood. The main brace lumber block was the dimension of eight inches wide, eight inches deep, and eight feet long. There was also a shorter block used which was the same dimensions with the exception of only being four feet long. We also used smaller four-by-four blocks for additional support.

To get the lumber supports to the higher part of the arch a *scoop* was used. The scoop is like a cherry picker, but not as high, with the steering wheel and driver on the left side of the vehicle, and an eight-foot bucket attached to the front. This contraption could be loaded with enough supplies and workers to get us to the higher parts of the arch for the purpose of bracing.

The engineers would determine where the arches were placed. Because of the placement of the arches, the space between the roof and the arch varied throughout the mine.

When I was at the very top of the arch, concern for my and others' safety was foremost in my mind. Working on those arches, placing the supports, only the unbraced roof of the mine above you, a lot of things run through your mind. Things like: *If this roof falls, we'll be buried under all this rock.* Or, *What if I slip while bracing this arch? Will the coal dust cushion my fall?*

While shoring up the bottom of an arch, I always had one thought that made me shudder. Some of my co-workers indulged in chewing tobacco. *If one such co-worker was working at the top of the arch, would I get spit on by accident?*

Everything from the roof to the arches was supported by laying the galvanized aluminium plate first, then lumber blocks. Your entire shift was underground. When break time arrived, your sitting spot was carefully chosen. You wanted to be sure to pick a safe spot where no rocks would fall while you were eating.

Keep in mind, in some areas the only light you had was that which came off your headlamp. Some areas had a little more, but not enough to make much difference when it came to picking a spot. It was so dark in the tunnels you couldn't see what you were eating.

All of us who worked underground packed extra in our lunches; those who went home with empty lunch cans didn't pack enough. There were no washrooms, porta-potties, or running water for personal use. If you shone your headlamp on whatever you were eating, it was black from the coal dust.

As part of the initiation for new members of the arches crew, Ted Deane always brought the new recruit a bottle of his specially prepared hot sauce for consumption. Being the new guy, I was required to eat it, and to my surprise it was really good sauce.

During my first week on the arches crew, a cave-in occurred. The mine roof had fallen in; we were required to remove all the rock off the roadway and set arches up. We were installing arches all that week.

Next on the agenda, a water line (pipe) needed to be placed on the wall in the Belt tunnel. The pipe had to be extended from the Main Roadway of the mine to the Belt tunnel. Before the pipe could be placed, a crew would have to dig out the designated (by the engineers) area of the mine in which the water and arches were to be placed.

After the area was dug out, and to assist in the installation, a small bulldozer was brought in. When everyone on the crew was asked if they knew how to operate the bulldozer, all replies were in the negative. Since I'm good with motor-driven vehicles, I volunteered to operate the small dozer—it couldn't be that hard, right?

After briefly experimenting with the dozer, I was successful in operating it and we could get on with the task at hand. The dozer was very useful to pull the pipes from the Main Roadway to the Belt tunnel where we were required to hang them. If we hadn't had the small dozer, we would have had to pull the pipes by hand, but because of this machine we were able to do the job in half the time.

Many areas deep within the mine were difficult to access because of the coal dust on the roadway. Officially the small dozer was only allowed in the areas where fresh air was readily available, but sometimes we utilized it deeper inside the mine.

The majority of the crew members, when scheduled for deep in the mine, taped the top of their workboots to their pant legs. Because of the depth of the coal dust, this was a way to keep the dust out of their boots. There was nothing more uncomfortable than having to work a full shift with a boot full of coal dust.

The essential piece of equipment used inside the mine on a daily basis came in three parts. The front part was called *continuous miner*, the middle part the *shuttle car*, and the one on the end was the *feeder-breaker*. The three sections were detachable and could be used independent of each other.

Another invaluable piece of equipment was the *boom truck*. Basically the truck was a flatbed with a hydraulic boom, but adjusted for mine use. Underground, the boom truck carried all the supplies to crews. It was so versatile that it could reach all areas within the mine. Without it, supplies couldn't reach the crews in the various areas of the mine; without supplies, the required work wouldn't get done.

There are many, many memories that are embedded, and upon reflection, brought me to the realization just how dangerous working underground in the mine was.

I was in the North Main tunnel (off the Main Roadway) one day. A fellow miner was driving the shuttle car and running over the power cable. There was a big blue flash and then everything shut down in the tunnel. They had to repair the cable by running a new cable from the power box to the shuttle car. Once the cable is damaged, the entire cable has to be replaced.

One day while working in the Southwest area of the mine (installing arches), work was halted. The tunnel, which had previously been prepared for the arches to be placed, was flooding with water. Because of the flood, the engineers had to pick another place in the Southwest tunnel to work.

CHAPTER 2

CAVE-INS

"Shifts at Westray for underground workers were 12 hours in length. In scheduling these shifts, Westray was in violation of section 128 (1) of the Coal Mines Regulation Act. Twelve-hour shifts increase the risk of injury and accident to the workers because of their mental and physical fatigue."
—THE WESTRAY REPORT

JANUARY 1992

DURING THE PROBATIONARY PERIOD, SHIFTS WERE SUPPOSED TO BE eight hours. Probation periods varied from worker to worker, and mine lasted three to four weeks. There were two tunnels to the mine: the Main Road and the Belt tunnel. After a couple of weeks working the day crew, I got moved. I was now a member of "C" crew, working night shift, and on the boom (supply) truck. The mine's shifts rotated among the four crews, named A, B, C, and D.

I worked four days on and four days off. The job was to take supplies down to designated areas of the mine. Supplies were to be placed as close as possible to the crews working at the various locations underground. To support the roof we would use what we called *cage wire*. It was an industrial-strength wire, which came in sheets. The sheet of wire would be placed on the area that was to be contained.

Using a bolter, the wire is held in place, several holes are drilled, a tube with cement-like material is placed into the drilled holes pushed up into the roof as far as possible, then a bolt is pushed into the tube of material. As the material is drying, a plate is fastened on the bottom of the tube to hold the tube and bolt over the wire sheet in place.

The bolter is capable of doing all the functions to secure the cage wire to the roof. Because the area that needs to be secured is vast, two people on either side are needed to ensure the equipment gives the desired results. The outcome is that loose rock is secured by the wire sheet.

January was bad for moisture running down the walls onto the roadway and causing muck. Also, driving the supply truck meant a lot of back and forth over tunnel roads, which created even more muck. This muck had to be cleared so that the various vehicles wouldn't get bogged down. During the day there were extra people, so someone was always available to clear the roadway of muck. During night shift it was a smaller crew, so we didn't have any extra people. Because I was the driver of the supply truck (for that shift), the supervisor asked me to take the responsibility to make sure the tunnel road was clear. All that was required for this task was to start up the small bulldozer and move the mud off to the side.

In January, the temperature was colder on night shift than it was in the day. It might be 20 degrees Celsius below outside, but down in the mines, because of the fans, double that. Some nights it was so cold that to get warm I would park the dozer and position myself between the blade and radiator to get heat from the engine.

The Main Road of the tunnel was very cold. The fan located at the Belt tunnel entrance would suck air from the main entrance to

Miner Carl Loveman operating the scoop at Westray in 1992.

the mine and expel it into the Belt tunnel. This method was used to circulate fresh airflow throughout the mine.

Some of the crew, when coming out of the mine after a shift, would wrap plastic around them to keep warm while sitting on the tractor, which would take them to the surface.

FEBRUARY 1992

When working in the Southwest area of the mine, because the coal dust was so thick, the dozer was required. The dozer was utilized to push the boom truck up the tunnel. Without that push, the work supplies for the shift could not be delivered to the site as required.

One particular overtime shift in early February sticks out in my memory. Supplies were urgently needed in the Southwest area. Robbie Doyle, Harry [last name not recalled], and myself were instructed to deliver them via the boom truck. I was on the passenger side of the boom truck with Robbie driving. Because of the accumulation of dust on the roadway in the Southwest area, Harry was instructed to follow behind in the dozer to push the boom truck when needed.

The progress to the Southwest area was slow. At one point, I happened to look over my shoulder. Behind us on the tunnel road were moving lights, as if another tractor were pursuing us. I recognized the approaching tractor immediately because of the unique placement of lights on the fender. I knew it was Roger Parry, the underground mine manager. When Robbie stopped the boom truck, the other tractor pulled up alongside us.

Upon closer inspection, we realized someone was riding shotgun with Roger. The tractor Roger always drove was a one-seater. On this day, Roger had a passenger who was perched alongside him half on the fender and half on the seat beside him. The visitor was none other than Albert McLean, mine inspector for the provincial government. [Both names would later play a significant role in the Westray inquiry into the disaster.]

Roger yelled, "What the fuck you guys doing with that dozer in this area? Get it the fuck out of here now."

This was confusing to all of us. Earlier that morning, Roger had instructed Harry to follow Robbie and me (in the boom truck) with the dozer to make sure the supplies arrived to the men working in the Southwest area.

Shrugging his shoulders, doing what he was told, Harry drove the dozer out of the Southwest tunnel and up to the surface. Following Harry's lead, Robbie and I followed Harry out of the tunnel in the boom truck. Robbie, Harry, and myself were in the waiting area, where miners on shift waited before entering the mine, awaiting further instructions as to how we were going to get the supplies to the workers in the Southwest area.

Several minutes later Roger appeared in the waiting area minus Albert McLean. Roger said, "Get back down to the Southwest area with the dozer and boom truck. The men are waiting for their supplies and can't begin work without them." That said, he turned and left. Realizing the inspector had left, it was back to business as usual and we proceeded back to Southwest tunnel with the dozer and boom truck.

As described earlier, the boom truck had a boom to lift heavy items. It was difficult operating the boom underground in the dark. Some areas had better lighting than others, but the majority of the time the only light we had to work by was on our hard hats.

Because of the difficulty working the boom truck in the dark, two people made the job safer for the operator of the truck, but that was not always an option. Operating the boom alone was very dangerous. Five to seven deliveries underground was a normal shift. Overtime was readily available. You didn't have to wait for overtime to be offered—you just went in on your days off and reported to the shift supervisor who then put you to work where needed. Personally, I took advantage of this method of overtime quite often.

Towards the end of February while working an overtime shift, I was instructed to bring the dozer to the North Main. The coal dust was accumulating heavily on the road in front of the mine face and had to be removed. The crew that cut the coal from the mine face kept getting stuck there because of the heavy accumulation.

I arrived at the North Main face with the dozer. Once there, over and over, I would drop the blade, pull the coal dust back, then push the coal dust off to the side of the tunnel. While performing this repetitive task, sparks were emitting from the exhaust pipe of the dozer.

Being mechanically inclined, I was getting nervous watching the sparks. My immediate supervisor could see the sparks as well. Wanting to get the job completed so the crew could continue extracting the coal, he encouraged me to keep going until the entrance was reachable for the crew. What I didn't realize then, but I now know, was how dangerous this practice was. The sparks put everyone in the North Main (including myself) in danger of an explosion.

March 1992

Another overtime shift, this time working in the Southwest area. I was assisting with the erecting of arches in this section. My job was operating the scoop while two men were in the bucket up high working on the arches. I was given the signal by one of the men in the bucket, via his headlight, to bring the bucket to ground level. While I was in the process of decreasing the altitude of the bucket, another light began shining at me.

With the light shining at me and someone shouting, "stop, stop," I stopped the bucket in mid-air. I was approached by the supervisor for that crew and asked, "What the fuck? What are you doing? You coulda killed me!"

Underground, the visibility was poor; being inside a vehicle made visibility even worse. The supervisor was under the bucket that I was lowering, and I didn't see him there. It's a huge responsibility controlling any machine underground and being aware of everything and everyone around you is hard to do.

When working overtime, you were placed wherever the extra body was needed. If (in overtime) you could get placed in different areas with various tasks, the more versatile you became. The more versatile you were, the more overtime was available to you.

Another overtime shift I was placed on the *bolter*. This was my first time on this piece of equipment. On this shift I was considered a spare while learning how to operate the equipment. It wasn't long before I had the knowledge of its operation down pat. I now could add the bolter to my resumé.

Overtime again. This time the shift was short an ill worker. I was chosen by the shift supervisor to work the *miner*. I expressed my concerns about never having used this equipment before but was willing to learn its operation.

The shift supervisor escorted me down to where the miner was located on that particular day, showed me what to do, then departed. I was entrusted to look after the cable on the miner and to make sure the driver of the miner didn't run over the cable.

If the cable was run over and cut, then that area of the mine would be shut down for repairs and the shift was lost. It was a big responsibility and the compensation reflected this. The driver of the miner was the highest paid of the mineworkers, and the *lookout* (which was what I was doing that day) was second highest.

Here I was only three months on the job, and I was training for the second-highest-paying job in the mine. Roman had said there was good money if you were willing to work, and no truer words were said than those.

One of the downfalls of working in the mine was a cave-in. From what I've been told, the rock underground in this area was not solid, but fragile. Therefore, when the earth shifted, the rock would disintegrate thereby causing the roof and walls to collapse.

Cave-ins occurred on a weekly basis, and by the end of March and into April there were some doozies. One example of a particular cave-in was when I was working a regular shift and it was shift/crew change. It was customary for the crews coming on shift to wait until the crews coming off shift were completely out of the mine. The tractors transporting the crews out of the mine were the same ones used to transport the miners down to the tunnels.

My crew was in the waiting area ready to head down. When the outgoing crew arrived safely at the waiting area, we headed down to start our work day. Our area that day was in the Southwest section, but we couldn't get to our designated work area because a cave-in had occurred after the outgoing crew had arrived in the waiting area.

It looked like a disaster area—there were steel beams scattered all over the roadway. These were remnants of what looked like several arches. They were so twisted they looked like pretzels. In amongst the twisted beams were rock, dirt, and lumber. The roadway was impassable and had to be cleared before we could access our designated work area for that shift.

—❧—

SECOND THOUGHTS

"The miners, supervisors, and underground tradesmen at Westray were not provided with adequate training in safe underground work practices. They went into the mine with little or no safety orientation."
—THE WESTRAY REPORT

APRIL 1992

Another overtime shift, this one on a Friday night with two other men. We had to erect some arches to replace the ones that had fallen down several days before. Because of the height required for these arches to work, we had to restructure from the traditional arches used. This required building scaffolding with a walkway underneath—like what a painter would use for high places—so workers could easily

These coveralls were part of the Westray display at the Museum of Industry in Stellarton set up to commemorate the tragedy.

walk through the area. That night when I arrived for the shift, I can remember looking up and saying to myself *O-MY-GAWD*—there was a big hole in the roof of the mine.

Randy Facette was the OHS (occupational health and safety) representative for the workers, and that night was also our supervisor. Once the scaffolding was built, we began to erect the arches with plates and blocks. That particular night we were using a cutting torch to burn holes in the arches in order to bolt them together. Concerned, I asked about using a torch underground, and Randy said it was okay to do so. So, taking him at his word, I continued on with the work at hand.

The third member of our crew that night was the same guy that I had met during my initial tour of the mine. I remembered him (unfortunately not his name) because back then he had asked me if I was crazy wanting to work there.

Break time was fast approaching and I could see some rock falling. I was extremely worried and a little scared. Trying to reassure me, my co-worker said, "Don't worry about falling rock unless you hear little pebbles; then watch out!"

We stopped for a break, then went back to work around 3:00 A.M. We had only been working about half an hour when I could see a circling light. The light was meant to attract my attention; that accomplished, I was then told to get out of the way.

We backed away from the area where we had been working. We could hear more rock falling—only this time pebbles were also falling. I turned and started running down the road of the tunnel. My heart was pounding, thinking, *This is it—I'm going to die in the mine.*

Meanwhile, my individual light source had fallen off my hard hat. I had to keep a tight grip on the light from the hard hat so I could see the roadway I was running on. Tripping and falling was not an option—the hard-hat light was an important piece of equipment to have at this particular time.

Running and trying to keep a tight grip on my light to see, I spotted another circling light in front of me, so I stopped. It was Randy and the other guy I had been working with. They asked if I was okay. I told them, "I'm damned scared." The dust was still heavy. We had experienced a cave-in. Because of the heavy dust, it was difficult seeing in the tunnel.

I wasn't moving, my heart was still pounding from the run, and I was still scared. We waited a little while for some of the dust to clear, then they walked back up the tunnel. I stayed where I was to see if the area was clear. It was determined that we couldn't work in that area until an assessment was done. Randy (nor the other guy) didn't have the authority to determine how dangerous it was or wasn't. It was a management decision as to whether that area could be worked.

Around 5:30 A.M. Roger appeared and began his assessment of the cave-in. I don't know about the other two, but I was anxious to go home after that shift. I wasn't interested in any overtime that week. It took a while to recover from the cave-in I'd just experienced.

When I went back into the mine to work my regular shift, I was more cautious and aware of my surroundings. Every little sound or rockfall would have me worried about another cave-in. It may have been old hat for some, but I was still spooked, which made me more vigilant than ever before.

The following week, I visited the tire shop and asked if my old job was still available. I had been replaced by Wayne MacLeod and another guy was hired to fill his job. Things were working out well at the tire shop and they weren't looking for any replacements or new employees. I asked them to let me know if there were any openings and left it at that. There was nothing more to be done.

I was hesitant to discuss my concerns and fear of the cave-ins with my immediate family. Needing to get it off my chest, I decided to confide in my wife's uncle George. After making him promise that it was just between us, I began confiding in him. We talked about the dangers working underground, my fears of another cave-in (that I wouldn't walk away from), and my concerns for my family if something happened to me.

Uncle George was a lifesaver to me. He was a good listener, didn't judge, didn't force his personal opinion—basically he saved my sanity in anything having to do with the mine. During one of our private conversations I told him that I had tried to get my job back at the tire shop, but the position had been filled and they had no other openings. I also shared with him my need for employment. I had to support my growing family; quitting the mine was not an option unless I could find employment elsewhere. Pictou County does not have a lot of well-paying jobs, and the ones that are available are few and far between. Because the good jobs are so few, anyone that has one of those remains until retirement.

A week went by with no cave-ins. I was still concerned, but breathing a little easier. Also, I had my confidant to keep me sane and on track.

FAMILY MINING HISTORY

My family is rich in miners on both sides.

The author is shown outside an open-pit mine in Stellarton. His family worked in many mines, but Westray was his first.

MY MOTHER'S SIDE

Grandfather Roy Oliver's entire working career was in the mines. Roy worked at the notorious Springhill mine (in Springhill, Nova Scotia). It had two explosions: one in 1956, which killed thirty-nine miners, and the other in 1958, called "the bump," in which seventy-four perished. My grandfather moved back to Pictou County after the first explosion in Springhill. Upon his return to Pictou County, he found employment at the Drummond mine in Westville.

Roy's brother George (my great uncle) also worked at the mine in Springhill before returning to Pictou County and gaining employment at the Drummond mine.

Roy's other brother Henry (also my great uncle) worked his entire mining career at Drummond.

James E. Taylor (my great uncle by marriage, known to friends and family as "Dix") was also a miner. As far as I know, he was employed for many years at various mining locations throughout Pictou County. Late in the fall after the Westray disaster, my mom was visiting and we decided to go see Uncle Dix. With the disaster still fresh, our conversation turned towards mining and Westray. Uncle Dix didn't know that I had been employed at Westray and how close I had come to being one of the miners left underground. When I told him about what had happened at Westray, he became upset and his voice got deep with emotion. With his hand on my shoulder he said, "If I had known you were one of the miners, I would have walked over there, gone down and grabbed you by the scruff of the neck, and pulled you out of that hole."

MY FATHER'S SIDE

Wilfred Theriault, Jr. (my uncle) worked at the Prince coal mine in Sydney Mines, Cape Breton, for over thirty years (his entire mining career) until he reached retirement age.

Albert Theriault (my uncle, my dad's twin brother) worked in the coal mine in Sydney Mines as well. During his employment at the mine, a workplace injury forced him to come out of the mines and into the "wash plant." Because of a heart attack, he was forced to retire from the mines after approximately sixteen years of service.

CHAPTER 3

DUST AND DANGER

"A coal mine can be quite 'forgiving' with respect to other aspects of safety, as long as the ventilation system is properly planned, efficient, and conscientiously maintained. The other major requirement of coal mine safety is control of coal dust, through strict clean-up procedures and regular stone dusting."
—THE WESTRAY REPORT

APRIL 1992

I RESIGNED MYSELF TO HAVING TO STAY PUT FOR THE TIME BEING until I could find other permanent employment. I was working my regular shift one day when I was approached and asked to stay beyond my shift to do stone dust. This was something I had never done, or had seen being done since I began working in the mine. Management informed me that they had a mine inspection coming up with the Department of Labour, and this needed to be done to prepare. Curiosity got the better of me and I committed to staying for half the shift.

That day the stone dusting was done in the Belt tunnel. My understanding is that it was supposed to be done throughout the mine. The purpose for the dusting was to stabilize the gases emitting from the raw coal. When in the mine before extracting the coal, the area to be extracted is sprayed with what was called limestone, which was a white powder substance. The limestone is then placed in bags weighing approximately fifty pounds each. I can remember upon my initial tour of the mine seeing those bags and thinking that they looked like raw concrete.

The limestone was then put into a large mixer (much like a baker uses when mixing large amounts of flour). A large hose was attached to the mixer with a spout for spraying purposes. This was a two-man operation, one man pouring powder into the mixer and the other using the hose to spray throughout the tunnel, including the walls and roof.

The transformation was incredible after the stone dusting. It looked so clean. I remember the guy I was working with that shift saying that this should be done every day. As far as I know it wasn't being done in the areas I was working every shift. I wouldn't have been so surprised at how clean the mine looked if it had.

This was the first time I saw stone dusting done. I had been working in the mine for months and upon seeing this procedure I began asking myself, *Are there more procedures that should be done that I haven't seen, and is it safe to be working in this mine if they're not being done?*

Shortly thereafter, I was talking to some of my co-workers. I was hoping to find an experienced miner in the group. One man was from Cape Breton and had worked briefly with my father. That particular area of Nova Scotia has a rich history in the mining industry. He had a long history of working in various mines throughout the province.

The story he shared was at a mine in Sydney Mines. My father had obtained a job at the coal mine where this man was employed at that point in time. My father worked the scheduled shift and never returned. Apparently, that was not uncommon in the mines. The work can be gruelling and not everyone is cut out to do it.

I discovered there were several men who were experienced coal- and rock-mine workers. Upon this discovery, my thoughts were, *There's experienced mineworkers here. If something wasn't right, they wouldn't be here, would they?* Some of my fears diminished, but they weren't gone completely.

One morning the crew and I were getting ready to go into the depths of the mine. As usual, we walked out of the waiting area and climbed aboard the tractor. The area we were working in that day took about fifteen minutes to get to.

As we were waiting, I reflected on another day when I was waiting to go underground and someone was trying to get on our tractor with a power saw. The worker with the power saw wasn't allowed to take the saw underground. I remember thinking to myself, *if a power saw isn't allowed, then why is a cutting torch?* The cutting torch used underground contained oxygen and acetylene. I didn't say anything; I just shook my head. For days at a time there were oxygen and acetylene tanks lying against the wall at the Number Ten Crossover.

April 1992

Another week in the mine. I was working my scheduled shift (not overtime) with my co-worker Mike Dooley. On this particular day, my duties included delivering supplies to the North Mine area.

Mike was driving the boom truck; I was riding shotgun. Both boom trucks have no doors and are high enough inside that you can stand up while driving. At this point in time, Mike was backing up while I looked on. Because light is limited in the tunnels, having two headlamps trained behind the vehicle is better than one. Suddenly the boom truck came to an abrupt stop.

I whipped my head around to look over at Mike, wondering why the abrupt stop. He wasn't at the wheel. I jumped out of the passenger's side and rushed over to the driver's side. I found Mike lying on the road writhing in pain. Because I was watching the back while Mike was backing up, I didn't see what had happened. Apparently, while backing up, Mike was leaning out the door of the truck.

He must have misjudged the distance and got jammed between the boom truck and another machine beside us. I hurried down the tunnel of the mine on foot to get help. Luckily the other miners were not working far away from where the accident took place.

Mike's injuries were serious and he was taken to the hospital via ambulance. This left me working alone on the boom truck the rest of the day. The next day when I came in to work my scheduled shift, I got the update on Mike's condition. Management didn't know how long he was going to be off, so they didn't replace him, which left me on my own.

Resuming my duties from the previous day, I loaded the boom truck. Mike was still off with his injuries, and no one was assigned to replace him, leaving me on my own for the second day. Starting the boom truck I proceeded down into the mine to make my supply deliveries.

Going into the various areas of the mine unloading supplies by myself made me uncomfortable. Always in the back of my mind was, *What if I have an accident? How long will it take someone to find me?*

The following week, my next scheduled shift, the crew and I were prepared to begin work, and waited for the crew we were replacing to arrive with the tractor. The other crew arrived, disembarked, and got ready to go home.

We arranged ourselves on the tractor and headed underground. Our destination that day was the North Main. Driving to our assigned work area, we observed that a majority of the road had caved in. I surmised that this must have occurred during the changing of shifts, when no one was there to see it happen. If the outgoing crew observed it happening, they would have reported it to the crew replacing them, so the incoming crew would be aware of the dangerous condition of the road and proceed with caution.

What a mess—the arches were twisted like a pretzel. It wasn't the first cave-in I had seen, but it was one of the worst. Several of us stayed behind to clear the roadway and build new arches, while the rest continued on to the assigned work area.

The author, right, shown with Robbie Doyle while working at the Westray mine. Doyle was one of the miners killed in the 1992 tragedy.

It seemed to me that cave-ins were becoming more frequent lately. There had been several and it was only the middle of the month. Previously to this particular cave-in, I was working another overtime shift at Ten Crossover. A friend of mine, Larry Bell, was working nearby on the belt crew. Larry and I weren't always working at the same time, so it was a treat to have a fellow hockey fan to chat with at break time.

During lunch break we got together and talked about hockey. We both played together on same team in the Stellarton Nova Hockey League. The conversation wasn't only about hockey; we also talked about our jobs, if the mine was a safe place to work, and family. Just normal break-time conversation.

Larry, who was from Eureka in Pictou County, had no mining experience before Westray. Along with Robbie Doyle, his would be amongst the first bodies found in the mine during the rescue just a short time later. Robbie, at just twenty-two, was the youngest miner lost, and Larry, at twenty-five, the second youngest.

Although the wages were good and there were lots of hours available to work, downtime was important too. I couldn't quite leave work at work. There would be times when I was at the Stellarton Rink and Larry would be there. Sometimes, like me, he would go to the rink right after work to blow off steam. We had a code—anyone who worked at the mine would understand it. If you didn't work at the mine, the signal would go unnoticed. All we had to do was catch the other person's eye and give a sign. A head nod meaning a cave-in, a headshake meaning no cave-ins that shift.

Looking back now, I don't understand my actions. I suspected the practices inside the mine weren't safe, yet I still put in lots of overtime. Who could have foreseen that it was going to blow up? My worst fear was that I would get buried alive underground; fire and being burned to death were a close second.

Another hobby of mine is car racing. In Antigonish, Nova Scotia, there's a racetrack not far from my residence called Riverside Speedway. I've enjoyed and participated in this hobby since 1981. At this racetrack, I met and became friends with Roy Feltmate, who later became a miner at Westray. He was only thirty-three when he was lost in the disaster.

Working still another overtime shift, I realized Roy was working that shift too. At break time, Roy and I sat together and the main topic of conversation was our mutual love for racing. As we were talking, I brought up the subject of the mine being a sponsor for local race-car teams. I asked him if he had approached management about a sponsorship for his team. Since it was the beginning of the season and cars were just being considered for racing, I figured I had plenty of time to get sponsorship. Because of the events that later occurred in May, neither of us asked.

That same day that I was working the shift, word came to us that we were changing our work area in the mine. The reason for the change was because of frequent roof falls and the floor was rising as well. These conditions were considered extremely dangerous and the area unworkable. Supplies had to be removed—that was my task for the shift, and however many shifts it took to get them moved. There was a lot of money tied up in those supplies, so it was essential that they all be moved to another area of the mine.

—✍—

MY LAST SHIFT UNDERGROUND

"The evidence before this Inquiry relating to the dust, gas, and roof conditions at Westray is unequivocal. The accumulations of both dust and gas and the state of the roof were extremely hazardous and menacing for all of Westray's short life."
—THE WESTRAY REPORT

MAY 1992

Spring was in the air; it was the beginning of May. I lived close to the mine, fifteen to twenty minutes on foot, and on nice days I preferred to walk. I enjoyed the warmth and sunshine during the walk, and it also gave me a chance to prepare myself for the twelve hours underground. I was working my regular shift that week and looking forward to four days off.

There was an abundance of overtime to everyone who was willing and able to work. If you were unable to work due to illness, appointments, etc., there was no call-in procedure, you just didn't report to work. For overtime the method was simple—just go to the mine, prepare to go underground, find a shift supervisor, inform the supervisor you were there on overtime. It never failed; there was always work somewhere within the mine.

I was on my four days off and not scheduled to work until Saturday, May 9. On Friday, May 8, I decided to put in some overtime. All ready to be assigned to a crew, I was in the waiting area when I spied Larry Bell. He was just finishing up his shift. This was his third night shift after being on all days previously. He informed me he was back for one more night, then it was his scheduled four days off.

Knowing I had a little time before being assigned work, Larry and I attempted to arrange a time convenient for both of us to get together with the other players from our hockey league. Voted by the Stellarton Nova Hockey League players, Larry had won the most sportsmanlike player for the 1991-1992 season. We needed to get some league and award winners' pictures taken for publication in the sports section of the local newspaper (formerly known as the *Evening News*).

Meanwhile, one of the shift supervisors requested that I take one of the scoops underground. A member of the regular crew was running late, so I filled in until he arrived on-site. When my replacement arrived, I was teamed up with another member of the crew, and we were issued another scoop.

Off one of the roadways in the North Main, a wall had been completed, basically making that part of the roadway a dead end. Using the scoop's bucket, we were to retrieve leftover supplies from the completed wall, and move them to another work area. When we arrived at our destination, the scoop's engine died. We attempted several times to restart the scoop but it wouldn't start. It didn't make sense to load the supplies in the scoop's bucket if the engine wasn't working.

Wanting to complete the task assigned, we walked from the side roadway onto the Main Roadway and waited for the supervisor to appear. We knew he wasn't far away and would be returning to the Main Roadway shortly. When he appeared, we informed him the scoop's engine quit just as we arrived at the wall. Using the internal phone system (only management was allowed to use it underground), he contacted the garage above ground. One of the mechanics brought another scoop down to us.

The non-working scoop had to be removed and returned to the surface to be repaired. With all of us working together, we hooked a chain on the non-working scoop and pulled it away from the wall and out onto the Main Roadway. The working scoop was then placed by the wall, and we were ready to load the supplies into the bucket.

With the non-working scoop now on the Main Roadway, the mechanic had to figure out a way to get it to the surface for repair. Thinking he had nothing to lose, he attempted to start the engine. It caught on the first try. Some of the scoops were equipped with sensors that would automatically turn off the engine if high amounts of methane were detected. The engine had cut off because we were attempting to use the scoop at a dead end (no airflow). The replacement scoop had a non-working sensor; therefore, little to no airflow didn't make a difference to its operation.

Keeping the replacement scoop with us, we moved it into position so that we could began loading supplies in the bucket. The supplies that needed to be moved that day were a cement mixer and numerous bags of cement. These items had been used to seal off the roadway. The roadway being cut off meant the airflow was limited and I could feel the change in the air; I was starting to get light-headed. I worked as quickly as possible, and within a short time the bucket was loaded and ready to go.

The destination for the material was number Eleven Cross cut. My instructions were to leave the scoop and its loaded bucket at that location. On my way to complete the task a miner [machine] was being moved down the roadway. The miners have the right of way, so the road was blocked. Not knowing how far the miner was moving to—it was close to quitting time—I prepared myself for a long wait. It's hard to believe, but my entire overtime shift that day was moving cement from one part of the mine to another.

The miners [machines] are not gas driven. They are powered by an electric cable located behind the miner. There are several power boxes along the roadway, and moving a miner from one location to another, depending on how far down the tunnel the new location is, could be a long and time-consuming process. The power boxes were roughly five hundred feet apart, so the miner could only go five hundred feet at a time. Every five hundred feet, the cable in back of the miner would have to be unhooked from the power box, walked five hundred feet to the next power box, and re-hooked. This was done repeatedly until the miner was at the desired location.

Because of waiting for the miner to be moved, I missed the shift-change tractor going back to the surface. Now I had to wait for the new crew coming into the tunnel on the tractor. When the new crew finally arrived, I asked if someone could be made available to take me back up to the waiting area/changing area, as I had already put in twelve hours overtime and was done for the day. I was taken to the surface, did my end-of-shift routine, and was headed for home. It was 8:45 P.M.; I had arrived at 7:30 A.M. My work day was finally over.

That night I didn't get a chance to talk to Larry because I was late getting out of the mine. I'd missed the tractor taking workers out. He would have been on the other tractor taking workers into the mine; thus our paths did not cross. I took a mental note to myself, saying that I'd talk to Larry in the morning to confirm our picture-taking arrangements. I'd be beginning my regular schedule, and he'd be finishing his, which meant he was going into his four days off.

CHAPTER 4

TRAGEDY STRIKES

"Methane is a dangerous pollutant present in coal. Although non-toxic, it is hazardous because of its flammability. It will explode in concentrations of between 5 and about 15 per cent by volume in air, and it reaches maximum explosiveness at about 9.6 per cent."
—THE WESTRAY REPORT

MAY 9, 1992

BECAUSE I WAS GOING INTO A DAY SHIFT, WHICH MEANT 8 A.M. TO 8 P.M. for four days, I followed my usual routine the night before which included an early night. I was awoken by the shrill ringing of the telephone. Still half asleep, I glanced at the clock to see it was only 5:30 A.M. Wondering who would be calling at such an early hour, a little irritated because I had to be at work in a couple of hours, and not wanting Marilyn (my wife) to be disturbed, I answered.

The voice on the other end was my sister in-law, Roberta (Bert) MacKay. She was relieved that I had answered. Much later, she revealed to me that she was so worried it would be Marilyn who answered and she didn't know what she was going to say if that had been the case. Bert lived a short distance from the mine and could see the road leading to it from her front window. She told me that she had been awoken to the sounds of sirens, and they were headed straight for the mine. Trying to ease her worries and also still half asleep, I told her it's probably no "biggie," just another minor cave-in or someone got hurt.

Hoping to reassure her, I told her I was on day shift and would be heading into work at 7 A.M. I'd find out what had happened and let her know. It was only 5:30 and I wanted that extra hour of sleep. Just as I was lying back down, Marilyn asked who was calling so early. I nonchalantly said, "Your sister; she woke up to sirens heading to the mine." Hoping both of us could go back to sleep, I told her I'd see what was going on when I got to work. That said, I went back to sleep.

Just as I was drifting off, I recalled a recent cave-in, when someone had been buried under rock and was taken to the hospital with injuries via ambulance. In the mine we had what we called an *ambulance tractor*. The ambulance tractor consisted of a regular underground tractor with a stretcher attached. Previously when a cave-in and injury occurred, I was the tractor driver and returned the injured man to the surface where a traditional ambulance was waiting to take him to the closest hospital. I discovered much later that the man buried was a close relative of Bert's husband. To my knowledge, she was not told of this incident.

It seemed like only a few minutes and the alarm was blaring. My four-day, twelve-hour work week had started. I performed my usual routine of getting out of bed, bathroom, and downstairs to eat breakfast. Lunch was made the night before, so I retrieved my lunch can and headed out the door.

As if it were yesterday, I remember that particular Saturday morning. It was 7 A.M. and usually the birds were singing and traffic was moderate. My back door faces Foord Street and overlooks the corner of Bridge Avenue and Plymouth Road (this area is known as Blue Acres to Pictou County locals). In early spring, the leaves are just beginning to engulf the trees and I have a full view of the roadway. Plymouth Road is the roadway that leads to the mine.

The weather was wet and foggy, and the area surrounding my home was eerily quiet. Deciding not to walk that morning, I chose to drive. Vaguely remembering the early-morning conversation with my sister-in-law, my eyes were drawn towards Plymouth Road. I saw flashing red lights and quickly got into my car and headed in that direction.

Seconds later when I approached Plymouth Road, I was unable to enter and proceed on to work. Two RCMP cars with lights flashing blocked the road to get to the mine. Naturally, because I could go no further, I stopped. One of the RCMP constables approached my car and asked if I was heading to work, to which I replied in the affirmative.

The constable informed me that was not possible because sometime in the early-morning hours the mine had exploded, and only emergency vehicles were allowed to use the road. To this day the only way I can describe my reaction to this statement was complete and utter shock. All the blood left my face. It felt like a big brick had just hit me square in the chest. So many questions and emotions were running through me that I can't remember responding to the constable.

I vaguely remember being instructed on where to park, and blindly following the constable's pointing finger. Upon arriving at the assigned area, I discovered that several of my fellow miners were already there. I could see that my shock was reflected in all their faces. It was difficult to comprehend that the mine I had been working in just eleven hours ago had blown up.

The Esso service station was where we were instructed to park our vehicles, and we all came together in a huddle, sharing what little information we had about the explosion. A short time later we were moved from the service station to the Plymouth Fire Hall which was located not far from the mine site.

Aerial photo of the Westray mine after the explosion, showing the devastation.

The "B" shift was underground at the time. Some of the men I knew socially, some I knew from the mine, and some I had never worked a shift with at Westray. Because of the way the time books were kept (the supervisor had a clipboard with names of who worked and submitted it at the end of the shift) numerous phone calls had been placed. Fellow miners and families of miners were gathered at the fire hall, with more arriving by the minute. The place was in chaos, very little information was available, and everyone was waiting to hear what had happened at the mine. Worry was etched in the faces of all who were there. The worry was there from getting the early-morning phone call, very little information, hoping that no one was hurt, or even worse, missing.

Finally the management that was at the fire hall gave some information about the explosion, and it wasn't good. The miners who were present at the hall were asked to volunteer in a rescue attempt. I don't remember raising my hand to volunteer but it was one of the first to go up. Not knowing what the rescue attempt entailed, I didn't hesitate because I knew that if it were me, the other miners would be there. No matter what crew or shift you were on, all the miners were a team and could be counted on to help out in an emergency situation.

Meanwhile at the fire hall, everyone was crying and hanging on to each other for comfort. The information given was so sparse that people were concerned about what was happening at the mine and why a rescue attempt was necessary. Once we were acknowledged, myself and the other volunteers prepared to go over to the mine site.

A van was in the parking lot waiting to take us to the mine; they didn't want numerous personal vehicles congesting the roadway. At the entrance to the mine road stood a two-storey house with blue siding. I mention this because it was the first thing that caught my eye upon entering the roadway—the once-blue siding was now black. It had been covered in soot from the explosion; my fellow volunteers also commented on the amount of black soot on the house.

Next thing I saw was another roadblock with RCMP patrol cars. Looking back, I didn't realize Pictou County had so many patrol cars—maybe they borrowed some from surrounding areas. The van parked in front of the mine office. We got out and hurried into the changing area. There was chaos here as well. Because of the extra people involved in the rescue attempt, lockers were at a premium. We were instructed to follow the routine of getting ready to go underground, but were to meet in the waiting area for further instructions.

There was general confusion in the locker area—more people than usual were there, several conversations going on at once, and a sense of urgency was in the air. Following the routine of preparing to go underground, I took off my street clothes, put them in my locker, and proceeded to the dry area. Once there, I unlocked my basket, pulled it down, and dressed in underground clothes. After getting dressed as instructed, I went to the waiting area. The rest of the rescue workers were gathered here, and we were awaiting further instructions.

While waiting I remembered that a telephone with an outside line was in the room, so I decided to call Marilyn. This would be the first time I'd spoken to her since leaving home. Because I had taken the early-morning call from Marilyn's sister, I wasn't sure if she knew about the explosion. Marilyn's Uncle Donny (Corning) had beaten me to the punch and had called her shortly after I had left for work.

When I informed Marilyn that I had volunteered to be part of the rescue crew and was going underground, she was alarmed. Apparently she had diligently been watching the news reports, relatives were calling, and the general consensus was that the mine could blow again. Mistakenly thinking it would reassure her, I said her Uncle Alex was part of the crew I was going underground with. Her reply with an elevated voice was, "Who in the fuck do you think he is: God? If the mine's going to blow again, there's nothing he can do about it!"

My wife, concerned for my and the others' safety, did not want me going underground. Again, trying to reassure her, I promised to call every time I returned to the surface. Because the information session was starting, I ended our conversation with that promise. The session started with what had happened early that morning underground. It was confirmed that an explosion had occurred and, shortly after the explosion, our *draeger* teams sounded the alarm. Although it was unspoken, we knew in our hearts that some of our people were trapped.

CHAPTER 5

THE RESCUE

"The conditions in the mine were terrifying. The force of the explosion resulted in severe instability within the roof and walls of the mine. Rock falls, of varying degrees of intensity, were almost continuous. Signs of the devastation were rampant, as were signs of impending danger...The poisonous, unbreathable atmosphere and the actively "working" ground surrounding the mine openings, with the attendant grinding and cracking, were extremely stressful. Yet these men, miners trained in mine rescue, each wearing his personal life-support system, went unquestioningly into that perilous environment with the hope of finding some of their comrades alive."
—THE WESTRAY REPORT

MAY 9, 1992

A *DRAEGER* TEAM IS MADE UP OF PEOPLE SPECIALLY TRAINED TO secure a mine area that has exploded. As a rule, there is more than one team with this special training within each mine, and there are several teams located throughout the province. Depending on the severity of the explosion, the draeger teams have the authority to call in extra teams. We were told that our explosion was severe and other teams had been called in to assist our draegermen.

The volunteers (myself included) were called *barefaced mine rescuers*. We did not have oxygen tanks or masks, just the self-rescuer, which we had been given when first hired, belts with miscellaneous tools attached that we used on a daily basis, and, of course, our lighted hard hats.

Because our draegermen knew the mine, they were split up and distributed amongst the out-of-area draegermen, so a larger area could be covered in a shorter amount of time. Time was crucial. One of the more experienced draegers was appointed coordinator of the entire rescue effort. His only responsibility was to document the progress of each draeger team when it exited the mine. This was an important but time-consuming process because the draegers could only enter one team at a time. The teams were only in the mine for a short period of time—they would exit, then the next team would enter. Much like a tag team in wrestling.

After the alarm had been sounded and the draeger teams assembled, work began underground. The draeger teams were already in place and working, as the barefaced mine rescuers (me included) were brought up to date on the draegers' progress.

Long before we got there, the draeger teams had been underground preparing the *crossovers* so that we would be able to safely access the roadway in the rescue attempt. Crossovers were large steel doors placed across from each other intermittently throughout the Main Roadway. Crossovers permitted easy access to the other side of the roadway and also helped to restrict the airflow throughout the mine. They were like an average door going into a house only made of steel. Some were large enough that machinery could pass through, and to access these it was like opening a garage door.

The draeger teams were making a rough pathway to get to each crossover. At the crossover, the draeger team, complete with oxygen tanks and masks, would erect two-by- fours of lumber, then cover the lumber with plastic. This was done very roughly to establish

Rescue workers waiting to go into the mine.

airflow and would be reinforced by the barefaced mine rescuers who would eventually follow the draegers after each crossover was made reasonably secure.

When we were finally permitted to enter the mine, the draeger teams had gotten to Number Six Crossover. Number Ten Crossover was where the rescue station was to be established. Having the station set up here made perfect sense. Number Ten Crossover was where the Main tunnel branched off into the North Main and Southwest tunnels.

There was a very slim chance that anyone was in the tunnel before Crossover Ten, but it had to be checked. All rescue workers surmised that it would be the North Main or the Southwest section that survivors (if any) would be found. It was with great urgency that all resources possible were used to get a clear roadway to this point as quickly and safely as possible. Barefaced mine rescuers were prohibited from going beyond Crossover Ten.

As mentioned above, the crossovers had huge steel doors at each end, but after the explosion these doors were just part of the massive debris on the roadway. When we arrived at each crossover we reinforced the structure the draegers had placed to establish airflow.

Our first responsibility was to further clear the roadway of debris, in order to get to each crossover, starting with Number One Crossover. To strengthen the plastic-covered structure we would encase the plastic with plywood, then (for more solidity) beginning at the bottom we put four-by-four blocks all the way to the top of the tunnel roof.

On the way to the first crossover, I can remember thinking to myself, *This is what hell looks like. What a mess.* Immediately after that was, *How could anyone have survived this?* Knowing I had to keep going, I pushed these thoughts out of my head and tried to concentrate on the task at hand. This was no easy feat upon seeing the devastation the explosion had caused.

All the barefaced mine rescuers were working together as a well-oiled team and we were quickly securing the structures the draegers had roughly built and clearing the roadway of debris in between the crossovers. The debris consisted of pieces of steel, machine parts, huge chunks of wood, rock, coal, and dirt.

While carrying out my assigned task, I thought back to my previous shift. I recalled there being two large transformers off to the side of the tunnel between Numbers Five and Six Crossovers. When we arrived at that location during the clearing of the roadway, the transformers were no longer where I had seen them last.

All the debris we encountered was shifted to the side of the roadway inside the tunnel. We wanted to clear the roadway as quickly as possible in order to reach Number Ten Crossover. After the roadway was cleared well enough for vehicles to pass, the plan was to return with tractors and remove the shifted debris from the tunnel.

On the first day of the rescue effort all the barefaced mine rescuers had for equipment were our personal tool belts, which included the self-rescuers. As we progressed further into the mine, we were upgraded to a Dräger Oxy-Sr60B Self-contained Self-rescuer. This piece of equipment was much larger than our self-rescuer, and couldn't be attached to our tool belt. I don't recall how I transported it with me, but I do remember it was heavy.

Arriving at the mine site at approximately 10 A.M. Saturday, we worked non-stop into Sunday morning, taking very few breaks, clearing debris. Because we were underground and working so hard to clear debris, time stood still. I'm not sure when we reached Number Ten. I do know it was late Saturday night or early Sunday morning.

Once the tunnel roadway was reasonably clear to Number Ten Crossover, the rescue station was established. Now the heart of the rescue effort began. The rescue station was the start-and-return point for the draeger teams. As stated above, the teams could only go in one at a time, so the team coming out would update the team going in as to how much progress had been made.

Each team, at its turn, would pick up where the previous team had left off. Their main objective was to look for bodies and ascertain how safe it was to go further into the tunnel. It was a long and time-consuming process that seemed to take forever, when in reality each draeger team was only in the uncleared part of the tunnel for a short time.

Community support for the rescue workers was overwhelming. I can't express my appreciation enough to the individuals and businesses that supported our rescue efforts.

Whenever I took a short break and arrived at the designated rest area above ground, there was an abundance of food laid out. It seemed to me that everything you could possibly want was available to eat. Sent from restaurants and individual kitchens, food was not scarce. There were also new boots, gloves, jackets, and chewing tobacco for the miners.

My heart was touched on Monday when children from the local schools contributed drawings for us. When the drawings were

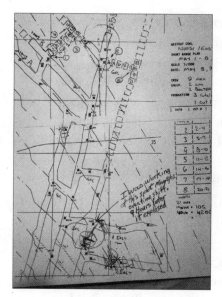

A drawing of the mine with the author's notation as to where he had been working.

received, they were promptly placed on the walls in the rest area for all to see. To this day, the drawings still exist and are part of the display at the Museum of Industry in Stellarton, Nova Scotia. These children would now be grown, and if they wonder what happened to their pictures, they have only to visit the display to see them.

Such overwhelming support from the community gave me (and I'm sure others) the strength and determination to keep pursuing the rescue effort. Rest was elusive. Every time I tried to close my eyes for a short rest, I could see my fellow co-workers who were missing. This image would push me to go back underground in the hope that I could make a difference and help to find the missing miners.

An important part of the rescue effort was transporting the draeger teams to and from the rescue station after the roadway had been reasonably cleared to Number Ten Crossover. Because of all the hours and different tasks I had performed within the mine, I was an obvious choice for one of the tractor drivers.

As I was performing my duties of transporting the draeger teams to and fro, I was gleaning tidbits of information with each journey. As stated above, one member of each draeger team was local and felt comfortable sharing information with me. Listening carefully to what the draegers were saying gave me the feeling that I was in the tunnels with them. With each trip, the picture was getting clearer as to what was happening beyond the crossover. What I was hearing and putting together wasn't encouraging for the miners trapped inside the tunnels.

The most notable passenger I had on my tractor during one of these trips underground was Elmer MacKay, who was a cabinet minister in the Mulroney administration. (MacKay, who represented the federal riding of Central Nova, is the father of Peter MacKay.) I mention this now because later on in this narrative, during the judicial inquiry into the Westray mine disaster, I talked to Elmer MacKay during a break and was primarily responsible for him changing his statement to the inquiry. I was able to correct his memory of details involving his tractor drive into the mine.

In the Southwest tunnel section of the mine, non-surviving miners were being discovered. At this time, I was asked if I would take the bodies to the surface on my tractor. I was hesitant, but reluctantly agreed. Shortly thereafter, I was informed that plans had changed. The bodies thus far discovered would be brought to the surface under the cover of darkness in deference to the families of the deceased.

Identifying the deceased miners would not be easy. Similar to the military, each miner was supposed to have been issued a *tag* to be worn around his neck on a chain. These tags were never issued at Westray—therefore identifying the deceased miners had to be done by other means. Management had a general idea of which miners were in which tunnel, but primarily the clothing worn was used for identification.

Shortly after the first of the bodies had been discovered, large dark-coloured bags with zippers were placed at the side of the tunnel. They were located just before the Number Ten Crossover, not far from the entrance to the North Main and Southwest branched-off tunnels. Those bags became a permanent fixture, and my eyes automatically went to them on every trip I made underground thereafter.

Late Monday afternoon, I was approached by a coordinator of the barefaced mine rescuers. He strongly suggested that I go home and try to get some rest. I hadn't been home since early Saturday morning and had been going non-stop. I agreed to go home in a little while; I wanted to help with the rescue as long as possible. It was between 5 and 6 P.M. before I finally arrived home.

CHAPTER 6

THE RESCUE ENDS

"Owing to the devastating nature of the explosion, the mine rescue efforts proved ultimately futile. No one in the Westray mine in the early morning hours of 9 May 1992 survived for more than one minute following ignition of the methane. The ensuing rescue operation demonstrated the bravery and dedication of the mine rescuers who rallied so quickly in support of their lost friends, fellow miners, and neighbours."
—THE WESTRAY REPORT

MAY 9, 1992

ONCE HOME, I HAD SUPPER WITH MY FAMILY AND TRIED TO WIND down. I was overtired and thought that watching some TV might help. Watching TV was not a good idea—all the local stations were showing the Westray mine explosion. The constant rehashing and updates were relentless.

Deep down, I knew I was exhausted. I needed to get some rest in order to return to the mine and the rescue effort. With this goal in mind, I retired to my bedroom and lay down. Sleep was elusive, and after an hour or so, I gave up and decided to return to the mine. Nothing much had changed in my absence; it was like I had never left. The only difference was that the Southwest tunnel had been, for all intents and purposes, cleared.

Looking back now, I don't know how I was able to keep going. I was functioning with very little sleep. My main objective (I'm sure everyone else's as well) was to get to the trapped miners as soon as possible. The draeger teams were now working on the North Main. This tunnel proved more challenging than the Southwest. According to the information I was receiving, the tunnel was smoke-filled with small fires burning throughout.

Because there was more severe damage in the North Main than in the Southwest, this part of the rescue effort was even more dangerous. The draegers were forced to make very small holes and slowly inch their way into the tunnel. I take my hat off to these men—they tried their hardest to clear both tunnels in the days following the explosion. I'll always remember the look on some of the draegers' faces when they climbed on my tractor for the ride to the rescue station. Less than a week after the explosion, and the rescue effort had begun, a meeting was called.

May 13, 1992

The main crux of the meeting was that the rescue effort was being shut down. It had been determined that it was too dangerous to continue. I (and I'm sure others) was severely disappointed. My first thought was, *Why is the rescue effort being called off so abruptly?* Then I realized that the dangerous conditions had come to a point that the rescuers would be put at unacceptable risk if the effort continued. I didn't want to lose any more people to the mine, so I acquiesced to the decision.

I don't recall how or when I got home that day. All I know is that when the shutdown announcement was made, it felt like my heart was being ripped out of my chest. I was unable to sleep that night and for many, many nights to come. Whenever I closed my eyes, all I could see was the destruction the explosion had made, and the faces of the miners that were left behind. Eleven bodies were never recovered.

Shortly after the explosion occurred, a young Stellarton, Nova Scotia, native, Jennifer MacDonald, authored a poem pertaining to the disaster. I have included it below:

PLYMOUTH EXPLOSION

On May 9th 1992
26 Lives away it threw
For the Plymouth Explosion was felt as it tore
And rocked along the east river shore.

Never again young miners said,
I quit this job before I'm dead.
They knew it was blowing underground
As they begged their friends not to go down.

He who worked the dirt so free
and chipped the coal to where the be.
The heroes we never gave credit to
Who risked their lives for the work they do.

Right now while the families weep
The spirits roam down so deep.
Never shall this be okay
The 26 lives that it tossed away.

Beyond the heavens high above
We think of you with all our love
Pictonians feel beyond the dreams
If the men who's spirits are in the seams.

The author poses with three other rescuers who went underground to try to save the miners. Second from the right is Ron Cunningham, a barefaced rescuer. The other two men were draegermen.

THE LOST MINERS

John Thomas Bates, 56; Larry Arthur Bell, 25; Bennie Joseph Benoit, 42; Wayne Michael Conway, 38; Ferris Todd Dewan, 35; Adonis Joseph Dollimont, 36; Robert (Robbie) Steven Doyle, 22; Rémi Joseph Drolet, 38; Roy Edward Feltmate, 33; Charles Robert Fraser, 29; Myles Daniel Gillis, 32; John Philip Halloran, 33; Randolph Brian House, 27; Trevor Martin Jahn, 36; Laurence Elwyn James, 34; Eugene William Johnson, 33; Stephen Paul Lilley, 40; Michael Frederick MacKay, 38; Angus Joseph MacNeil, 39; Glenn David Martin, 35; Harry Alliston McCallum, 41; Eric Earl McIsaac, 38; George James Munroe, 38; Danny James Poplar, 39; Romeo Andrew Short, 35; Peter Francis Vickers, 38.

FRIENDS AND CO-WORKERS

Twenty-six men were killed that day. All had loved ones and friends. I knew Larry Arthur Bell from hockey. He was from Eureka in Pictou County, and if we were ever working on the same crew, we shared lunch breaks together. Robert (Robbie) Steven Doyle had no previous mining experience. I first encountered him when I delivered tires. He later trained me on the boom truck and I worked several overtime shifts on his crew.

I am not sure how much experience Roy Edward Feltmate had as a miner. Roy and I raced stock cars together for a couple of seasons in Antigonish. Roy's child and mine attended the same school so we would see each other at school functions.

John Thomas Bates was an *overman* of B crew, which meant that he was basically the shift supervisor. I knew him from work but had no outside contact.

Bennie Joseph Benoit was an experienced underground miner who had relocated from Cape Breton. I'm not sure how long he worked in the mining industry. I met him before I began working at the mine when I worked at the tire shop.

Eugene William Johnson was an experienced miner with nine years underground and eight years above ground. My first encounter with him was in my early teens hanging around the streets of Westville. I got to know him better in later years through my wife's uncle, Alex (Ryan). Eugene and Alex were as close as brothers and constantly in each other's company when not working.

George James Munroe was an experienced miner. I worked with his brother John at both tire shops and met George at one of the tire shop's Christmas parties prior to being hired at Westray. He was on a different crew but we worked together infrequently on overtime shifts.

Michael Frederick MacKay was a miner I knew vaguely from my youth in Westville. What stands out in my mind about Mike was me once walking in on a heated argument between him and Roger Parry (mine manager) just off the break room (where batteries were recharged and picked up before the start of each shift).

PART TWO

THE

AFTERMATH

CHAPTER 7

NIGHTMARES AND SURVIVOR'S GUILT

"The Westray Story is a complex mosaic of actions, omissions, mistakes, incompetence, apathy, cynicism, stupidity, and neglect. Some well-intentioned but misguided blunders were also added to the mix."
—THE WESTRAY REPORT

MAY 1992

AFTER THE MINE DISASTER, I WAS STRUGGLING WITH ALL ASPECTS of life. Trying to make sense of it all, I also knew my struggle was affecting my wife, children, and other family members.

The nightmares were constant and the survivor's guilt was intense. I kept turning over and over in my mind the events that had transpired in such a short period of time. Maybe I was still in shock— my foremost thought was that it could have been me trapped in the North Main. The explosion had happened between my shifts. Fate had determined that I wasn't supposed to be there when the explosion happened, but my heart went out to the families who had lost loved ones that awful day. When the mine blew up it killed twenty-six men. My life had been completely changed forever. I was a basket case, barely functioning at all. My wife and children were profoundly affected by my behaviour. They didn't understand why I would fly off the handle at the slightest little thing or not communicate at all for extended periods of time. My family, who know me well, were at a loss as to how to help me. I was so overwhelmed that I couldn't help myself. Unless you've gone through something this traumatic, it's hard to understand the dark place my mind was residing in.

Finally, in desperation, I made a doctor's appointment. Our family doctor had been replaced by Dr. Manoj Vohra, and this would be my first appointment with him. Dr. Vohra had arrived in Pictou County in February, and had taken my former doctor's patient load. I hoped against hope that the doctor could help me or point me in the right direction. Arriving at the doctor's office, I was unsure what his reaction to me would be. I was not myself by a long shot; he was meeting me for the very first time, and vice versa. I worried that he would think I was a nutcase and write me off. Normally I'm an easygoing guy who gets along with everyone, but these were not normal circumstances.

I'll always be grateful to Dr. Vohra—he was very understanding and compassionate with me. After discovering my role in the Westray disaster, he couldn't have been more helpful. Individual counselling was first on his list, then a support group of people with similar traumatic experiences when I was strong enough to share my story.

After filling out the required forms for workers' compensation, Dr. Vohra made an appointment on my behalf for a psychological assessment. With the Workers' Compensation Board (WCB) paperwork filed, I experienced a slight sense of relief. I wasn't going back to work at the mine anytime soon. That was fine with me, I would have been happy never to see the mine site again in my life. My mindset at that point was, *The mine site is hell on earth.*

MAY 21, 1992

Marilyn accompanied me to my first appointment with Steven Dunsiger, M.A., clinical psychologist. This was the psychologist that Dr. Vohra had arranged for me to see. The majority of the time was used to get my background and to see if I was comfortable enough with the psychologist to continue working together. Fortunately the psychologist was local and a good match for me. After the initial appointment, Marilyn saw that I was comfortable and saw no need to accompany me to further appointments.

JUNE 1992

I was seeing the psychologist two, sometimes three, times per week depending on the severity of my nightmares. The most recurring nightmare was that of a ball of fire hurling towards me. I would then jolt awake. The dream was so real that I would wake up screaming, lathered in sweat, heart pounding. Marilyn was afraid to sleep beside me because of the frequent and disturbing nightmares.

Throughout the summer months, I continued seeing my psychologist and Dr. Vohra frequently. One of the many tools that I was taught through these sessions was walking. I found it very useful and walked daily for over an hour and found it helped relieve some of the strong feelings regarding Westray that raged inside me. PTSD (post-traumatic stress disorder) was a concern for Dr. Vohra and my psychologist. Although I had not been officially diagnosed, PTSD was the elephant in the room.

Meanwhile, I began experiencing back pain. In the beginning it wasn't too bad, but as time went on it became worse. It was to also become a major issue in my mental healing process.

JULY 1992

I received a request, via mail, from the RCMP for a face-to-face interview regarding the Westray disaster. This caused me great concern. I was hesitant to discuss Westray with anyone because of the standard conflict-of-interest form I had signed when first employed

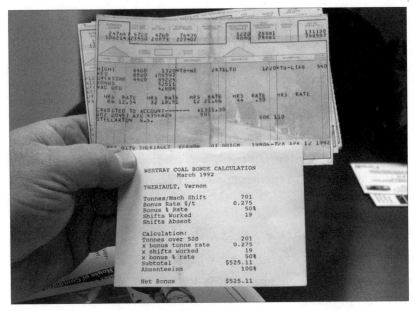

The surprise bonus that the author discovered after the disaster.

at the mine. Technically I was still employed at Westray, even though I was receiving workers' compensation benefits.

Not knowing the legalities of the form I had signed, I frantically searched for a reason not to attend the interview. Eventually, because I couldn't think of a good reason not to, I agreed to the interview. It had only been a short time since the disaster, and I was still trying to come to terms with what had happened. Talking about the mine only brought my frustrations and anger to the forefront. My nightmares were still ongoing and it seemed that my life was at a standstill.

Pay at the mine was bi-weekly and direct-deposited. The company had initiated a bonus program, which involved the amount of coal retrieved from within the mine. I had never received this bonus, thus it completely slipped my mind. Two months after the disaster I was talking with a fellow miner (my wife's uncle Alex). The topic of conversation came around to the bonus money. I assumed that the bonus, if any, was direct-deposited. Alex informed me this was not the case, and asked if I had my pay stubs. Upon retrieving the stubs and going through them, we found a cheque for $528.11 attached to a separate stub in the April paperwork. This was the bonus. Alex jokingly said, "You'd better hurry up and cash that cheque, the company's going bankrupt." Early the next morning, when the bank opened, I cashed the cheque.

A NEW ASSESSMENT AND A SETBACK

SEPTEMBER 3, 1992

WCB arranged a psychiatric assessment for me with Dr. Mark Rubens who was located in Dartmouth, two hours away. I was required to take this assessment in order to continue receiving benefits. Because I was already in therapy and comfortable with my psychologist, I was nervous about the interview with someone new.

From the very beginning, I was uncomfortable with Dr. Rubens. I had filled in several general information forms before the interview began. The interview had little to do with the disaster at Westray, but more to do with my childhood and family. During the progression of the interview I remember thinking, *What does this have to do with the mine blowing up and me losing friends and co-workers?*

After the interview concluded, I returned home and resumed my therapy and doctor's appointments, as if there had been no WCB intrusion into my recovery process.

Approximately the middle of November, I received a letter from the WCB. The letter was undersigned by Dr. Tom Dobson, administrator, medical services, WCB. As the medical representative for WCB, he had reviewed my assessment from Dr. Rubens, which had occurred in early September. His perusal of the assessment was not in my favour.

Two weeks later, in early December, I received another letter from WCB. This one was undersigned by B. MacAulay, claims adjuster, WCB. Basically what it stated was that my benefit claim was approved until December 28, 1992, and then would be closed. A booklet was enclosed on how to appeal the decision, but, as will be explained later in this narrative, I was unable to understand the procedure to follow. All I knew was that I was being cut off from WCB benefits and I wasn't even halfway through my recovery. *Merry Christmas, Vernon, courtesy of the WCB.*

I was devastated. It seemed that I had just reached my lowest point. I wished that I had been one of those guys lost in the mine. My will to live had just deserted me. The previous seven months had been wiped away and it felt like the disaster had happened yesterday.

My emotions were overwhelming and all-encompassing. The numerous cave-ins that had occurred when I was working in the mine, the blow-up just hours after I had left and before I was scheduled to work again, the five-day rescue effort with little to no sleep. Now a letter from WCB closing my file as of December 28, which basically meant all benefits were being cut off.

How could a psychiatrist who had seen me one time for one hour, with little discussion about Westray, say that all I was suffering from was adjustment disorder with some mixed emotional features? Looking back now, maybe I should have brought the discussion around to the disaster and opened up more. In my own defence, I didn't feel comfortable with this guy. Thinking he was the professional who knew what he was doing, I allowed him to take the assessment in whatever direction he chose.

Finally, in desperation, I made an emergency appointment with my psychologist. Thankfully, my family doctor and psychologist did not agree with the psychiatric assessment and urged me to appeal the WCB decision. Both were behind me 100 per cent and even went so far as to write letters to WCB on my behalf.

One of the benefits when appealing a WCB decision is that they supply you with a lawyer to argue your case. Shortly after, I was assigned a lawyer (Jill Graham-Scanlan); we met, and the appeal process began. I didn't realize how long a process this was going to be.

Knowing that I would have no income to support my family during the appeal, and being incapable of working due to my fragile mental state, I applied for employment insurance. At that time, EI took approximately four weeks (now it's eight weeks) to receive benefits. Because of my WCB appeal, when I applied for EI I was required to sign a form of repayment to EI if my WCB was successful. Not knowing if my EI claim would be accepted, I went to Community Services for help in the interim.

The social worker I was assigned to, Reggie Foote, was very helpful. Upon our initial meeting, I informed him of my circumstances. I was given a cheque to cover rent and miscellaneous bills that same day. I also signed a form stating I would repay any monies given if my EI claim was successful. We also discussed my upcoming appeal with WCB and he was confident that I would be successful with that also. Reggie was a wealth of information about ongoing education programs offered, and believed I was a perfect candidate for these programs.

JANUARY 1993

Numerous letters were sent back and forth between my lawyer, the WCB psychiatrist, and WCB. Meanwhile, I was getting frustrated. Not having done this before, I didn't know how much rigmarole went on. It seemed to take forever to get settled and I took my frustration out on my lawyer. I'd like to take this opportunity, Jill, to apologize for giving you such a hard time. I'm sure you probably explained the process to me but, at that time, I wasn't listening.

My goal at this time was to receive retraining, so that I could find suitable alternate employment. Attaining this goal would prove to be a challenge. Unbeknownst to my family and friends, and which testing later on would prove, I was illiterate. I was embarrassed and had managed to hide this disability throughout the years. Now I was in a position where I could correct it. I guess I always knew my reading and writing skills were poor, but until the test, I didn't know how bad.

MY EDUCATION HISTORY

Growing up, my family moved a lot so my education history reflects that. I started my academic career at Church Street Elementary School in Westville, but halfway through grade three our family relocated to Halifax.

The second half of grade three, I attended Tower Road School. Because I started mid-term at a different school with a different curriculum, I had to repeat grade three. During this time we had moved again (within Halifax to Allan Street), so for the second round of grade three I attended Chebucto Road School. Halfway through grade five, we again moved. This time to Cornwallis Street, but I was still able to attend Chebucto Road School.

The beginning of grade six I attended St. Patrick's-Alexandra School on Brunswick Street. Known as St. Pat's, it was a Catholic school taught by nuns (we were Protestant). The nuns were really strict and to this day I can still remember them walking down the aisles with a ruler ready to hit your desk or hands.

Shortly after the school term began, we again moved. I had been at St. Pat's for such a short time that I never experienced my desk or hands getting hit by the ruler. We moved to Mulgrave Park in the North End of Halifax, and I attended Richmond School on the corner of Kenny Street and Devonshire Avenue for grades six and seven. The Richmond School is now the home of the Supreme Court of Nova Scotia, Family Division.

Towards the end of grade seven we moved. I was failing at Richmond and I can remember myself and another student having to write our exams in the principal's office. We moved to Spryfield (a suburb of Halifax) and I enrolled in a new school, BC Silver on Pine Grove. There were only three classes of

The author as a young cadet in Halifax.

grade seven. Incredibly I passed grade seven and went on to grade eight, which was just the next building over and called BC Silver Junior High.

In grade eight at BC Silver Junior High, every Friday at lunchtime our class sponsored a sock hop. This was something I looked forward to and enjoyed very much. My marks were slightly better at this school. I believe I was doing better at BC Silver because I was more content there.

I passed grade eight and just before Christmas in grade nine I decided to quit school. I was struggling with the schoolwork and getting easily frustrated when I couldn't complete the assignments. Years later, my mom told me that she had a meeting with my grade nine teacher and between them they devised a plan to get me back in school. Mom also told me that my teacher had said, "Don't worry about Vernon, he will do good in life." I returned to BC Silver shortly after Christmas.

As an incentive, my grade nine teacher had arranged a work/study program for me. The work/study was with Sears in the warehouse. I can't remember if it was two days a week or one that I worked in the warehouse, but the rest of the week I attended school. I continued the work/study program until the end of the school year. It ended upon my graduation from grade nine.

Wanting to continue my education (with a work/study program) I began looking into schools that offered this. Queen Elizabeth High School offered a hands-on program, much like the old vocational schools. Mornings were regular schoolwork—English, math, etc.—and afternoons you were in the shop. The shops included machinist, carpentry, and mechanics. During the school year, the students would be in each shop for a third of the term, thus introducing them into all three trades. This appealed to me. I was accepted into the program and began grade ten in September of 1978 at QE High.

Around the end of October / early November, our family moved back to New Glasgow. The only school that I could find that offered close to what I was taking in Halifax was the Pictou Regional Vocational School (located in Stellarton), which had an adult program. I enjoyed the shop part but found the schoolwork hard. Shortly before Christmas I left school, this time for good.

My unsuccessful academic career cost me opportunities. When I was twelve, I joined Army cadets in Halifax. The Halifax chapter was located at the Halifax Armoury, not far from Citadel Hill. After over two years in the cadets I had worked my way up to sergeant stripes. The higher up you go in cadets, the more responsibility.

Because of my limited reading and writing skills, I felt I couldn't go any higher and resigned from the cadets. I was disappointed because I had received a high-score shooting trophy. My last year with the Army cadets I went on a six-week (in-house) training course at CFB Gagetown located in New Brunswick.

CHAPTER 8

REHABILITATION

"There is no question that management knew that the levels of methane underground at Westray were hazardous. Management was aware, or ought to have been aware, that, under section 72 of the Coal Mines Regulation Act, such conditions mandated the withdrawal of workers from the affected areas."

—THE WESTRAY REPORT

MARCH 1993

I FINALLY RECEIVED THE LONG-AWAITED CALL. WCB HAD DECIDED to reopen a claim on my behalf. The claim would be for rehabilitation, which was what I had hoped for. I was appointed a counsellor and we met for the first time at my home on March 16. The main topic during this meeting was what my goals were and what the rehabilitation would entail.

I reluctantly informed the counsellor of my reading and writing skills, or lack thereof. After my confession, I then shared the future I foresaw, with the proper reinforcement, for myself. I wanted to attain a grade twelve certificate and a viable trade.

The community college, for my purposes, in my area starts in September and ends in June. It was the middle of March so the first step in the rehabilitation was to have several written tests performed. These tests were done at the college itself to see where I would fit in. Several community colleges offer grade twelve equivalency as well as a trade at the same time. This was the category I was hoping to fall into, but testing proved otherwise.

APRIL 1993

I had performed two sets of tests at the community college. The first set on April 20 was the Test of Adult Basic Education (TABE). The second set on April 27 was Differential Aptitude Tests (DAT). I don't recall personally receiving the test results—I believe they were submitted to my WCB counsellor. The first time I laid eyes on the testing results was years later when my lawyer requested copies and forwarded them to me.

Adult Basic Education test (TABE's), written April 20, 1993, with the following results:

Vocabulary	3.4
Mathematics Computation	6.9
Language Mechanics	4.7
Comprehension	5.4
Mathematics Concepts	7.7
Language Expression	4.6
Spelling	1.8
Total Language	4.7
Total Reading	4.5
Total Battery	5.4
Total Mathematics	7.2

Be advised that these scores are expressed as grade equivalents.

On April 27, 1993, Vernon wrote Differential Aptitude Tests (D.A.T.'s) with the following results:

Verbal Reasoning	10
Numerical Ability	15
Verbal Reasoning & Numerical Ability Average	10
Abstract Reasoning	70
Mechanical Reasoning	15
Space Relations	75

These scores are expressed in percentiles with 50 being an average.

Yours truly,

The author's test results uncovered some challenges.

June 1993

It had now been over a year since the disaster at Westray. Normal every-day life was difficult, and I was doing everything I could to maintain some stability in my household. I was still having nightmares, and sessions with my psychologist had all but ceased. My concentration was now on education so I could provide independently for my growing family.

Disregarding my test results, my WCB counsellor decided to enrol me in a computer class. The class was in a private trade school in Antigonish, approximately forty-five minutes away from my home. Thinking this class would help prepare me for my upcoming attendance at community college in September, I made the daily trip to Antigonish. The duration of this class was two months and a WRAT-R (2) (Wide Range Achievement Test) was administered before and after. Like many of my generation, I had never used a computer before, but I tried my hardest to complete the required work.

September 1993

Having completed a two-month computer class during the summer, I was now at the community college campus ready to begin the next phase of my education plan. I had no idea how difficult and frustrating this endeavour would prove to be. Like all educational institutions, books were associated with the classes I was attending. Because of my illiteracy, the required books were useless and homework was impossible for me to complete. I paid close attention in class to make up for not being able to do the homework. I worked hard; I was determined to complete this goal in spite of my disability.

In November, after I had been attending classes for two months, my WCB counsellor paid me a visit on campus. The purpose of the visit was a forewarning of a letter I would be receiving from WCB. My vocational rehabilitation and academic upgrading would be terminated as of June 1994. At this time, I informed him of the difficulty I was having keeping up with the classes. The only remedying of the situation we could come up with was to schedule a meeting with the student counsellor whose office was located on campus.

The meeting was scheduled quickly, and all three of us were present. Basically, the outcome was that I would continue my education at an off-campus location, which offered the same curriculum but at a slower pace. The location change was to be effective immediately and by the December break I was comfortable in the new location. The student-teacher ratio was one-on-one and the class size was smaller. Although I still had the reading disability, the hands-on approach eased the workload somewhat.

The expected letter arrived at my home on November 18. It looked like another appeal to WCB was imminent. One year was not going to be enough time to attain the goal the WCB counsellor and I had set. I was having a hard time trying to comprehend why I was having to file yet another appeal with WCB in order to get the education I so desperately needed. My understanding of WCB is that it is a government organization set up for injured workers to rehabilitate themselves and that our taxes help fund this process. It seemed to me that with every step forward, I fell two steps back. With the assistance of my sister-in-law (Angela Lennon), I filed yet another appeal to continue the education process.

January 1994

My education appeal was successful. I would finish up the year in June, then re-enrol in September for another year. Deep down I knew I needed to further my education. My frustration level was about to reach its peak. Besides having to deal with WCB and the difficulties at school, I was still coming to grips with the Westray disaster and the loss of co-workers who were also friends.

The successful appeal to attend another year of school was my third appeal in eighteen months. When the WCB-appointed counsellor visited my home back in March of 1993, we had talked about my goals for the future. I distinctly recall confiding in him that my reading and writing skills were severely deficient. I also remember discussing that my goal was to attain a grade twelve diploma and a certified trade in order to adequately support myself and my still- growing family.

If I had known then what I know now, I would realize that I was placed in the wrong school from the beginning. My reading and writing skills had to be strengthened before I could attend the community college. Because I didn't know any better, this issue was dismissed by everyone, including me. With the added pressure I was putting on myself to attain my immediate education goal and the constant WCB appeals, my frustration level was again rising. Although almost two years had passed since the Westray disaster, I was still having nightmares.

The pressures I was dealing with were intense. Day-to-day life was not pleasant. Because of the pressures and nightmares, my sleeping habits were virtually non-existent. I wasn't eating properly, slept only in short spurts, constantly worried that WCB benefits would be cut off. Foremost in my mind was, what if my benefits were cut off—how would I support my family during the appeal process?

I found myself yelling at my children constantly and for no particular reason. On one occasion, during this stressful time, I was awoken from yet another nightmare by my wife. When I became aware of my surroundings, my hands were around her neck. I was choking her. She was afraid, crying hysterically, and trying to free her neck from my hands. Several years later, Marilyn confided in me that it wasn't the first time I had choked her while in the midst of a nightmare, but it was the worst. Needless to say, I was banned from sleeping with my wife for a long time. I will never forget that night, and will always be grateful to her for understanding the turmoil our lives had become.

My nightmares were vivid—when I did sleep—and I always awoke with my heart pounding and in a sweat. The nightmares were so real, as though I was actually there. I was still having the ball-of-fire dream in which I was helpless to stop it from consuming me and my surroundings.

—❧—

INNER DEMONS

"The Westray tragedy is regarded in the industry as a black mark against coal mining in general rather than a localized event."

—THE WESTRAY REPORT

NOVEMBER 1994

The spring and summer passed with me still dealing with my inner demons. WCB was quiet and my benefits continued. I was enrolled for another year at the community college, again in the off-campus classes. I was still struggling with the classwork, but the lower student/teacher ratio eased the load somewhat.

Early summer I received a letter from the governor general of Canada. I, along with other rescue workers from Westray, was to receive the Medal of Bravery. In total, two hundred men were to receive this honorary medal and Governor General Ramon (Ray) Hnatyshyn would personally present the medals to each individual. The protocol for bestowing such an honour to an individual or group was to hold the official ceremony in Ottawa. Due to the large number and because of travel, it was deemed efficient to hold the ceremony in Pictou County.

The chosen location for the ceremony was Sharon St. John United Church in Stellarton. Not everyone who was being awarded a medal was still in the Pictou County area, and therefore some could not attend. Some of these men who had relocated to other parts of Canada were flown in.

The ceremony began with a church service, followed by those of us who could attend being awarded the individual medals. The location of the church was adjacent to the local community college, which housed a fairly large-sized gymnasium. The reception (which was held in the gym) was a stand-up affair where people attending could freely move about. It was a bittersweet reunion for many of us. This was the first time that such a large group of us had gotten together since the mine disaster.

The author poses with Governor General Ramon (Ray) Hnatyshyn after receiving his Medal of Bravery.

JANUARY 1995

It had been thirty months (two and one-half years) since Westray. The nightmares were just as bad as when the disaster first occurred. To add insult to injury, I was still having difficulties at school. My non-existent reading and writing skills were impeding any progress. Only with verbal instruction could I make any headway. In my opinion, I was giving 110 per cent effort, but to no avail.

I was not getting enough rest due to the nightmares, my schoolwork was suffering because of the lack of reading and writing skills, and my back pain was increasing at a steady rate. My nerves were shot; I was stressing out with all that was going on.

Then the forbidden thought came into my head: *Enough already! I feel like I'm just spinning my wheels here! Nothing is coming together like it should! Why should I keep trying? I can't deal with my life the way it is anymore! Maybe it's time to end the suffering and just check out!!*

I thank God every day for my wife and kids. Their love and support for me gave me the strength to push thoughts of suicide out of my head and to forge ahead.

The author and his wife, children, and grandchildren in 2018 at the Westray Miners Memorial. Left to right: Aaron Theriault, Marilyn Theriault, the author, Lindsey Theriault, James Theriault, and in front: grandchildren, Kyle Theriault and Ethan Christopher. (Missing: grand-daughter Tori Fitzgerald)

February 1995

After nearly two years of school, I was required to schedule an appointment to write a GED (General Educational Development) test. The test took a little under two days to complete and was located in Halifax, two hours' drive away. My test was February 8 and 9, all day Friday and half day Saturday.

I put forth my best effort, but I knew in my heart that it was not good. Several weeks later my suspicions were confirmed—my marks were low. I didn't pass. Disappointed, a meeting was arranged between myself, Gerard Benoit, my vocational rehabilitation counsellor whom I first met in February 1993, and the counsellor at the local community college I had been attending.

I informed Gerard (for the second time) that my reading and writing skills were non-existent. Any home/classwork that required reading was impossible for me to complete. Verbally and hands-on were the only ways I was capable of learning.

Finally Gerard got it! He suggested I might want to try Mariposa Reading Achievement Centre located in Truro, a forty-five-minute drive away. At this point in time, I was willing to try anything if it would assist in achieving my goal of a grade twelve education.

March 1995

It was several weeks before I could begin attending Mariposa Reading and I was still attending the local community college as well. When I look back on those days, I wonder how I ever did it with so much on my plate.

April 1995

The first thing that was done when I began attending Mariposa was an assessment. The centre had to discover which grade level I was at in various subjects to determine what my course studies should be. The first set of testing was so low, the director of the centre asked me to do another kind of test (which was at a college level). After the second test was completed, the director requested a meeting. I was informed that because my score on the second test was so high, they could work with me to get the other subjects up to a grade twelve level.

There was a lot of work to be done. According to the first set of tests, the grade levels varied from grade two to low grade five (depending on the subject). I didn't know vowels or consonants (pronunciation) and I couldn't name any of the other provinces (besides my own) in Canada.

It was discovered during this testing I had a learning disability—dyslexia. Because of the dyslexia, my reading and spelling level was hindered. With assistance from the centre, I could be taught the tools of reading. It was hard work for both of us, but I was determined to succeed.

I found the days extremely long and tiring. For three months (until June) this was my weekday schedule. I would arise between 5:30 to 6 A.M. to get ready for the day. I'd leave my house around 7 A.M. and drive forty-five minutes to Truro for classes starting at 8:00 A.M. Classes lasted till noon, then it was drive back to New Glasgow (another forty-five minutes) for community college classes starting at 1:00 P.M. Community college classes lasted until 3:30 P.M.

By the time the weekend came, I was tired from all the driving and classwork. All I wanted to do was rest and get the energy together to do the same thing all over again on Monday. It was a good theory, but normal family life happens on weekends, and with a wife and three small children rest was scarce.

PURSUING MY GED

JULY 1995

The community college term was ending for the summer. I was hoping my tight schedule would loosen a bit. At this point in time, my lower back was painful and my mobility was suffering. It was suggested I get accommodations in Truro through the week to ease the long driving hours (and hopefully ease the pressure on my lower back). Also I would now be going to Mariposa full-time: 8 A.M. to 3 P.M.

My progress at Mariposa was steadily improving, and my instructor and I decided to give the GED another try in August. Because of the dyslexia, we requested through the Department of Education that I write a special GED test (designed to accommodate learning disabilities). This request was granted, and preparations for the test began in earnest.

We were working hard towards the GED because I wanted to enter a carpentry program at the community college in September. A grade twelve or equivalent was one of the main requirements for enrolment in this program.

AUGUST 1995

Test writing time had come! All my hopes and goals were pinned on passing this test. After writing the GED, I had to wait several days to get the results back. I was praying that I passed and could continue on with the goal of taking the carpentry course.

The results were in—I failed the GED by one point in an important subject and five points in a less-than-important subject. If only I had got that one point, I would have passed. Mariposa re-tested me. Although I had improved to a grade seven level in many subjects in a five-month span, I still had some hard work to do to get that elusive GED.

Because Mariposa knew how to work with dyslexia, and through hard work on my part, I was improving and my grade levels were rising. My confidence was increasing with each day and learning was even becoming fun, instead of frustrating. I was actually beginning to see a light at the end of the tunnel. All my hard work and sacrifices were not in vain. With Mariposa's help—despite dyslexia—I had achieved more in five months than in the thirty months since my rehabilitation began.

Things were just going too good, I guess. The next impediment in my development reared its ugly head. WCB wanted to end my claim, thus stopping the funds I required to run my household and continue my education. Apparently dyslexia has nothing to do being gainfully employed and they wanted to explore an on-the-job training program.

If I could find a company willing to hire me, WCB would fund the training. My back pain had not lessened. Because of the constant back pain, my mobility, as well as lifting and standing, were compromised. What company was going to want to hire/train someone with a bad back? Also, Pictou County does not have many large industries and employment opportunities are limited. There's a large workforce available, kids are graduating from area high schools and community college and don't have PTSD or excruciating back pain.

George Gasek, PhD, speech-language pathologist, and director of Mariposa, penned a letter to the WCB on my behalf. He requested that the board allow me more time at Mariposa until I could successfully obtain my GED. My lawyer, Jill Graham-Scanlan, also wrote a letter to WCB requesting more education before I was turned loose on the workforce with my limited skills. Basically, they wanted me to have a fighting chance with all the obstacles that were before me at that time.

Armed with letters from the director of Mariposa and my lawyer, I appealed the decision from WCB about continuing my education. I was turned down flat—the decision for on-the-job training was final. I had to hit the streets and find a company willing to hire me, or risk losing my only income. Knowing my options were limited, I decided to return to Bridgestone Tires, which owned Good-Wear, where I had been employed before Westray.

I requested a meeting with Donnie Aikens, my former manager at the tire shop. During the meeting with Donnie I explained my predicament. Although he was sympathetic, there was not much he could do. He said he was fully staffed and, as I knew, in January there was always a temporary layoff till business picked up in the spring. When I informed Donnie that WCB would pay my salary for up to thirty-two weeks, and as a favour to me, a position was created. The understanding between us, WCB representative included, was that at the end of the thirty-two-week period there would not be a permanent job.

CHAPTER 9

SURGERY

"The unsafe use of torches underground was a common practice at Westray. Management was aware of the practice, condoned the practice, and reprimanded those who condemned it."
—THE WESTRAY REPORT

SEPTEMBER 1995

WCB APPROVED A THIRTY-TWO-WEEK ON-THE-JOB TRAINING WITH Bridgestone Tires on my behalf. From the first day, I knew that at the end of thirty-two weeks I would again be scrambling for an income to support me and my family. Because of my chronic back pain, Donnie customized my work. Even with the modified work, I was unable to fully perform my job. Because of the constant pain, I was at home more than I was at work. My frustration was mounting—I was raised to believe that you put in a day's work for a day's pay, and that wasn't happening. My family doctor tried different variations of physiotherapy, as well as pain medications. Finally, in November, I was scheduled to see a back/nerve specialist located in Halifax.

The author at the microphone in Ottawa, asking federal MPs a question. On the left are Nancy Hutchison, Steve Hunt, and Harry Hynd, all from the Steelworkers.

(ABOVE) *Westray ballcap at the Museum of Industry in Stellarton.*

(LEFT) *Westray bolter at the Museum of Industry.*

The author at the Westray Miners Memorial in New Glasgow.

The author and Nancy Hutchison of the United Steelworkers.

Steve Hunt of the Steelworkers and the author at Peter MacKay's office in New Glasgow when MacKay was the local MP.

At the twenty-fifth memorial, from left to right, Alain Croteau, Nancy Hutchison, Ken Neumann, Lawrence McBrearty, Stephen Hunt, and Sylvia Boyce, all of the Steelworkers.

Men of the Deeps help commemorate the twentieth anniversary. The choral ensemble is made up of former coal miners from Cape Breton Island.

Allen and Debbie Martin at a Westray memorial in New Glasgow.

Peter Boyle, the author, Debbie and Allen Martin (Westray family members), and Del Paré. Allen lost his brother, Glenn, in the disaster.

The author with Leonard Bonner, a draegerman who went underground in the rescue effort. The men are shown twenty-five years later in front of the Westray Miners Memorial.

Family photo 2018 at the Westray Miners Memorial. Left to right: Aaron Theriault, Marilyn Theriault, the author, Lindsey Theriault, James Theriault. In front: grandchildren Kyle Theriault and Ethan Christopher.

The lobby group from the second time the Steelworkers worked the Hill in 2002.

A stained glass memorial to Westray.

November 1995

After exhaustive testing and a review of what my family doctor had done, the specialist determined that surgery was my only option to relieve the chronic back pain. A disc in my back was pressing against the nerve, thus causing pain and numbness in my leg. If I didn't have the surgery, my chances of losing my leg were huge. Already the muscles in my left leg were in atrophy.

Surgery was scheduled for some time in March. I was also put on a wait list, which means if a patient cancelled their surgery, I could take their place. Thinking I had five months to wait, I went back to everyday life. Imagine my surprise when I received a phone call in late December from the specialist's office saying I could have the surgery in the new year.

January 1996

Surgery was performed on January 2, 1996. As a result, I was unable to work for eight weeks. I was hoping the surgery was a success, but I found no difference in the numbness or back pain. I returned to the surgeon's office four weeks later for the mandatory post-op check. I expressed my concerns about the pain and numbness being no different than before the surgery. His explanation was that because of the damage to the nerve, it would take time to heal. Accepting his explanation, I left the office with the thought that I have to give it more time.

March 1996

Knowing that the on-the-job training with Bridgestone would soon be ending and wanting to get my GED, I decided to file another appeal with WCB to get my education back on track. In my opinion, employment at Bridgestone was a waste of time that would have been better spent at Mariposa getting my GED. My lawyer agreed with this assessment and together we filed the appeal. Despite our combined effort the appeal was denied.

APRIL 1996

Meanwhile, my chronic back pain and leg numbness had not improved. My family doctor sent me back to the specialist who did another scan. It was determined from the scan that the nerve was still pinched and further surgery was required. Another eight weeks wasted, but if it would ease the pain I was all for it.

MAY 9, 1996

Four years to the day of the mine disaster, I was in Halifax at the QEII awaiting my second back surgery. Before my turn in the OR, I decided to watch some TV. I couldn't believe my eyes—there was a news program on and it was featuring Albert McLean, the government mine inspector at Westray. Turning up the sound, I was shocked. The inspector was saying that he believed the explosion happened because of miners' errors. Shortly afterwards, I was taken to surgery.

The next morning when the surgeon was doing his rounds, he approached my bed and we discussed my surgery of the day before. He commented that the anaesthesiologist had experienced some difficulty putting me under, and had to administer additional anaesthetic during the procedure. I informed him of the news program I had watched before being taken to the OR. Then further explained the significance of the previous day's date. Once he heard the explanation, he understood why the difficulty had occurred.

—ço—

"The Department of Labour in general, and the inspectorate in particular, was markedly derelict in meeting its statutory responsibilities at the Westray Mine...It must be profoundly unsettling to the people of Nova Scotia to realize that the department's safety inspectorate is so demonstrably apathetic and incompetent."
—THE WESTRAY REPORT

June 1996

Despite all of my efforts and those of others, my benefits were halted at the end of June. The clock turned back to September 1992. I had no EI benefits to fall back on this time. I had to figure out a way to get some sort of income to support my family. My mindset was: *who would hire someone with two recent back surgeries?* I had to swallow my pride and return to the Community Services (welfare) office for assistance.

August 1996

After several consultations with my family doctor, we decided to apply for Canada Pension benefits. Although I was only thirty-five at the time, there's a provision in the Pension Act for persons disabled. The application process starts with the family doctor filling out the initial forms. The forms are submitted to the federal government pensions department, which in turn assigns a local caseworker. It's a long and arduous process. In the meantime I got a tip that Trenton Works, a local railcar building company, was hiring welders. Although out of practice, I was an experienced welder and had worked for that same company back in the '80s.

After the initial interview, I opted to re-familiarize myself with basic welding skills. Because I had previously worked for the company, the interviewer suggested I just relearn the basics. If I could get forty-five days continuous employment, I would be eligible to join the union. Union workers are the last to be laid off, then it's last hired first laid off. With the instructor at the local trade school's permission, I practised basic welding after school hours.

September 1996

I, along with five other former employees of the company, was hired. Now I needed to halt the pension process. My first stop was my family doctor, then on to the assigned federal caseworker. I was so happy to be employed. When I cancelled the application, I was told that if in the future I was unable to work, I could reapply.

Unfortunately, I only worked a total of thirty-eight days before being laid off. I was seven days short of the forty-five days continuous employment. Also because the time of employment was so short, I didn't have enough hours to draw EI.

NOVEMBER 1996

Back to Community Services I went. During this time, the inquiry into the Westray disaster was being held. It was headed by Justice Kenneth Peter Richard of the Trial Division of the Supreme Court of Nova Scotia, and the Museum of Industry in Stellarton had been chosen as the location. The museum was a fifteen-minute drive away. Wanting to keep abreast of what was happening at the inquiry and being unemployed, I was there practically on a daily basis.

At the railcar plant, we had a weekly hockey pool (during hockey season). In order to stay in the pool I visited the plant weekly with my filled-out sheet and money. It was during one of these visits that I came across a former manager from the '80s. We spent the first few minutes catching up with each others' families and then he asked if I was working. He mentioned that he hadn't seen me on the floor recently.

I informed him I was one of the ones recently laid off. Regretfully, he said rumour was that the most recent layoffs would not be returning for another eighteen months. Disappointed, I shared with him about being short seven days in order to join the union. I also said that I didn't know if I could use the time I was employed in the '80s to boost seniority. He suggested that I try going to human resources and see if they could somehow bridge my time.

That same day I went to the company human resources department and asked to speak with a representative. Upon reviewing my internal file, I was informed that on numerous occasions the company had tried to contact me. Apparently the company had tried contact through both letter and telephone—unsuccessfully.

Armed with copies of the file, I went home. When I started going over the papers again there seemed to be too few. Determined

One of the exhibits at the Westray inquiry.

to get to the bottom of this, I returned to the human resources department and asked if there were any more papers and/or files. This trip was more successful—another file was discovered in back of the file cabinet with my name on it.

This file proved more fruitful. A letter had been sent to me via general delivery (dated February 12, 1992) asking if I wished to remain on the seniority list at Trenton Works. I affirmed that I did, signed where indicated, and returned the letter in a self-addressed stamped envelope. I never thought anymore about it; then the disaster happened in May, and it completely slipped my mind. Now (four years later) I remembered signing the letter of intent, and realized how important it now is. It was like winning the lottery!

The correspondence showed that the company received the signed letter February 17, 1992. I was very diligent in sending changes of address and/or phone number to Trenton Works. According to the personnel files now in my possession, on May 21, 1992, a letter from human resources got sent to General Delivery, Westville, NS. Within the letter was an offer of employment (valid for a limited time). At this time I was residing in Stellarton and never received the offer. Subsequently (because of no reply to the correspondence) on June 12, 1992, I was terminated from Trenton Works.

The only explanation I can think of is that on one occasion when I submitted a change of address it was written on a sticky note and attached to my personnel file, then filed away. Sometime during this process the sticky note must have dislodged and my new address wasn't on file. Now I had written confirmation of why I was terminated. My next stop was to the local union office of The United Steelworkers of America (USWA) to see if there was anything that could be done to reinstate my seniority.

BACK AT WORK

JANUARY 1997

Several days later a meeting was convened. In attendance were myself, a representative from human resources for Trenton Works, and the president of Local 1231 United Steelworkers of America. It was determined at this meeting that because of the mailing error I would get my seniority back. The starting date for seniority purposes was June 4, 1981. Finally, after all the turmoil of the last five years, a decision was made in my favour quickly and with minimal effort.

I was once again employed with Trenton Works and my seniority was intact. A steady paycheque was coming in, bills were getting paid, and food was being put on the table. Everything was as it should be. When I was employed at Trenton Works previously, I was a welder. Again I was welding, but it wasn't the same as before. Too much had occurred in between.

After completing a welding task, I would remove the safety helmet and look at the spark of the weld. My recurring nightmares would return while gazing at the spark: fire was coming at me—out of the tunnel of the mine. I would have to shake off the thoughts in order to continue working. My family was counting on me, and in order to keep my sanity I had to battle through. At this time I was still consulting with my psychologist Steve Dunsiger for PTSD.

MAY 1997

Trenton Works built railway cars and my job (as well as several others) was welding them together. To us they were called *hopper cars*. Four to five men worked on a hopper car at one time (it was that big). Before entering a hopper car to weld, we had to put on what looked like a space helmet with a rope attached (oxygen hose). With that many people welding at one time it tended to get very smoky. It was an assembly-line process. In this process was what was called a *turn around*. Step one on the assembly line was put on the gear and enter the railcar. Step two was weld the right side of the car. Step three was the turn around. Step four was re-enter the railcar and weld the left side.

This was what I did eight hours a day, five days a week (not including overtime). During one of these shifts I injured my back attempting to enter a hopper car. When I put the safety helmet on, I didn't see that the oxygen hose was wrapped around my leg. So, when I tried to climb into the hopper car, I wrenched my back and fell backwards. To the average person, this is no big deal, but since I had had two back surgeries, it was a big deal for me. I was assigned light duty for a couple of weeks (to give my back muscles a chance to heal), then back to my usual work duties.

AUGUST 1997

It was the middle of August (the 15th to be exact) and I was going about everyday life, dealing as best I could with my inner demons. Out of the blue (or so it seemed) I received a letter from WCB concerning the injuries (emotional and physical) I incurred as a result of the Westray mine disaster. It had been over five years since the disaster, but to me it still seemed like yesterday.

An appointment had been made, on my behalf, with Dr. Judith Hammerling Gold, CM, MD, FRCPC, FACP, FAPA, located in Halifax on August 21. The allotted time for the consultation was one hour. After the initial questions were asked and the conversation started flowing smoothly, we went over the time by almost an hour. Marilyn had accompanied me to the appointment and waited anxiously outside the office for the session to conclude.

When the assessment was finally concluded, the doctor escorted me to her office door, and strongly recommended that I continue my therapy with Steve Dunsiger. She felt I still had multiple issues that had to be dealt with regarding Westray and the aftermath of said event.

Approximately a month later, I received a letter from WCB with Dr. Hammerling Gold's findings. According to the *Summary Report and Decision*, I did have PTSD. The findings were the result of my experiences as a rescue worker following the Westray mine explosion. I was assessed with a 35 per cent permanent medical impairment. Steve Dunsiger's diagnosis (shortly after the explosion) was confirmed by Dr. Hammerling Gold over five years later.

February 1998

Although I was a member of the union, I did not attend the regular monthly meetings. During a meal break one day, one of my fellow workers (a regular meeting attendee) commented that a position was available for an inside guard within the local union. What further piqued my interest was that as an inside guard I could also attend meetings between the company and union.

Feeling beholden, because the union had fought (successfully) to get my seniority back, I decided to attend a meeting. Also, I was curious as to what an inside guard's responsibilities were. After the initial meeting that I attended, I applied for (and got) the position of inside guard. Because of the position, I attended every union meeting thereafter, until July 2000.

PART THREE

THE
WESTRAY
BILL

CHAPTER 10

SEEKING JUSTICE

"Bill C-45, also known as the Westray Bill, was created as a result of the 1992 Westray coal mining disaster in Nova Scotia where 26 miners were killed after methane gas ignited causing an explosion. Despite serious safety concerns raised by employees, union officials, and government inspectors at the time, the company instituted few changes. Eventually, the disaster occurred."

— CANADIAN CENTRE FOR OCCUPATIONAL HEALTH AND SAFETY

MAY 1999

OUR LOCAL UNION PRESIDENT, DONALD MURPHY, ASKED IF I WOULD like to accompany him to Ottawa for a Steelworkers National Policy Conference in October. With such advance notice, I requested a couple of days to think about it before giving him confirmation. Upon arrival at home, I consulted with Marilyn. Never having been outside of Nova Scotia before and never having flown, I was nervous. When myself and the two hundred other mineworkers had received our medals, the officials had come to us.

OCTOBER 1999

On Sunday, October 24, I took my first plane ride. We flew non-stop from Halifax to Ottawa. From the Ottawa airport, we travelled to our hotel via taxi. The hotel was in downtown Ottawa within walking distance to everything. Don and I were sharing the hotel room and once inside we unpacked. I decided to play tourist and visit Parliament Hill, which was just around the corner.

I informed Don I would be back in about an hour, grabbed my bag, which contained my medal and various letters pertaining to the medal, and headed to Parliament Hill. When I arrived at the main entrance, the guard asked me, "Where are you going?" Remember, this was my first trip to Parliament Hill, not to mention outside of Nova Scotia. In my innocence, I told him, "I'm here for a visit on the Hill."

Imagine my surprise when the guard retorted, "No! You can't go in there." My reply was, "Why? I've got a Medal of Bravery that I received from the governor general in 1994 and an open invitation to visit *us* in Ottawa." *How was I to know that advance notice had to be given through my Member of Parliament?*

The guard then informed me that visitors had to make arrangements through their MP, and that I should contact mine. The MP for our area at that time was Peter MacKay.

Disappointed, I returned to the hotel. I re-entered the hotel room not long after I had left. Don saw the disappointment in my face and asked

A T-shirt that the author wore in Ottawa, showing his Medal of Bravery.

what was wrong. Don was then unaware that I had been employed at Westray. He also didn't know that I was a part of the rescue effort, and that I had received the Medal of Bravery. I then filled him in on my Westray past and told him of my intention to visit the Hill.

After my failed attempt to visit the Hill, and having experienced my first plane ride, I was exhausted and decided to call it a day. I was thinking that hopefully things would look better in the morning after a good night's sleep.

The next morning Don and I got up early, had breakfast, and headed over to the policy conference. During the first break of the conference, I was sitting in the hallway drinking water, and waiting for the next round of meetings to start. Unbeknownst to me, Don had been talking to some of the conference attendees. He told them that I was a former Westray miner and had been heavily involved in the rescue effort.

Minding my own business, drinking water, and looking around, I was approached by a couple. The woman was Nancy Hutchison (health and safety coordinator, District 6 USWA Ontario & Atlantic region). The man was Steve Hunt (health, safety, and environment-education coordinator, District 3 USWA British Columbia). Steve held this position from 1995 until 2004, then became director of USWA District 3 in April 2004. Once the introductions were made, I was peppered with questions about Westray.

Don had informed several of the attendees at the conference of my history with Westray, and the misstep that had happened yesterday on Parliament Hill. The next round of meetings was commencing so we returned to our seats. Lawrence McBrearty, Canadian national director of the Steelworkers Union, was the speaker for this part of the conference. Before he began his planned agenda, he introduced me to the room with a short account of my Westray history. I was Mister Popularity for the rest of the conference. During every break, I would have several people introducing themselves, shaking my hand, and expressing their sympathy concerning the disaster.

OCTOBER 27, 1999

The agenda for this part of the policy conference was for the delegates to walk (a quiet demonstration) on Parliament Hill. Previously I had been turned away from Parliament Hill and the Steelworkers Union was made aware of my disappointment. Wanting to make my first conference experience positive, I was asked to lead the walk. I gladly accepted the honour.

Earlier that year (in March) the House of Commons had passed a report of recommendations from Justice Richard on the Westray mine disaster. His report was highly critical of the mine operators and called for changes in provincial labour and mining laws and departments.

The Steelworkers' representatives and I had questions for the Members of Parliament. Since they were all gathered in one place, we decided to take advantage of the opportunity and pose our questions. The assembled MPs were split up into separate rooms (approximately three per room). The room where I was placed was full of people and

Justice Kenneth Peter Richard at the Westray inquiry.

The author with Alexa McDonough.

bright lights. Since I was the only one speaking in that particular room, all lights and attention was focused on me.

Bill C-259 had received first reading in the House on October 21, 1999, and had been introduced by Alexa McDonough (NDP-Halifax) as a private member's bill. [C-259. An Act to amend the *Criminal Code* (criminal liability of corporations, directors and officers.)] The basics of Bill C-259 was to change the existing laws and hold corporate officials responsible for workplace injuries and/or deaths.

When I stood to address the MPs, I was so nervous that I could feel my knees shaking and my voice trembling. The room was so quiet you could hear a pin drop. My all-important question for the MPs was, "What will you do to convince your party to support this bill and pass it into law?" In my head I was saying, *Stop another Westray disaster.* I was terrified but it felt good to get that off my chest.

The author with Peter MacKay.

After I delivered the question, I had to sit down; my legs felt like they were going to give out. Because of the tension and nervousness leading up to addressing the MPs, I don't remember their response. My mission was accomplished—I hoped I could get the deceased miners the justice they deserved.

Upon hearing about my aborted tour of Parliament Hill, my MP, Peter MacKay, gave me a personal tour. Later that evening, to release some of the stresses of the day, Don and I rented a car, drove to Montreal, and took in a hockey game. Montreal was only an hour away, and we didn't know when we would have this opportunity again.

Thursday was the last day of the conference. After all the excitement of the week, I was ready to go home. When I got home, life went back to normal. I resumed my regular routine, which included going to work on Monday.

After attending the conference I was eager for something positive to come out of the Westray tragedy, which had affected so many lives. No one was ever held legally responsible. This seemed like a chance to be part of a movement, which eventually inspired the rallying cry "No More Westrays."

[Charges, including manslaughter and criminal negligence causing death, were laid in 1993 against Westray's owners and two of its managers, Roger Parry and Gerald Phillips. But the prosecution later dropped the charges, saying it did not believe it had a reasonable chance of conviction. The handling of the case drew widespread criticism.]

—୧⁊—

November 1999

Life for me was back to normal—the conference in Ottawa was a month ago and a distant memory. Out of the blue I received a phone call from the United Steelworkers. Apparently, I had made a good impression in Ottawa because the Steelworkers were asking if I would return in May 2000 for a campaign. The campaign was called *Push for Legislation* and the goal was to have corporate officials who didn't follow proper safety guidelines liable for on-the-job deaths that could have been prevented.

I was to be one of the of the guest speakers along with Robert Ellis. Mr. Ellis lost his son, David, in an industrial accident his second day on the job in the Toronto area. David was only eighteen years old. Wanting to accumulate some funds before heading off to university in the fall of 1999, David had accepted employment with a small bakery. The second day at work he was pulled into an industrial dough mixer, and subsequently died. His family, to honour his memory, and with the assistance of the Steelworkers' Campaign for Young Workers, had become advocates in educating youth to work safely.

The agenda was to fly into Ottawa on Sunday, May 28, then fly home on Tuesday. The purpose of my attendance was for the kick-off of the campaign. In attendance would be Lawrence McBrearty, Robert Ellis, myself, and many others. Locally, Howard Sim from Trenton Works would be there for the campaign as well as for two weeks of lobbying at Parliament Hill while the MPs were in session.

May 2000

Howard and I flew to Ottawa on Sunday morning. Everyone attending the campaign and/or lobbying was scheduled to stay at the University of Ottawa dorm. The university was also where we were to all meet and receive our agendas of scheduled activities. After we had all assembled, we were assigned our rooms (as well as roommates). Not having experienced college life, I didn't know the rooms were so exposed and that privacy was at a minimum.

The majority of the group were not impressed with the accommodations and filed a grievance with the Steelworkers. After brief negotiations, we were moved to a hotel. Once we were settled in our rooms, it was close to suppertime and several of us were getting hungry. We decided to go down to the hotel restaurant to eat.

Just as we were finishing our meals, I was approached by Nancy Hutchison. Apparently I was supposed to be dining with Lawrence McBrearty, Robert Ellis, as well as herself. Nancy said it was all arranged and Lawrence was buying, so I had a second meal at another hotel.

At the second restaurant I was given the agenda for the kick-off campaign. The order of events was discussed and any changes made were finalized at that time. After another delicious meal, I returned to my hotel and turned in early. I anticipated a busy day and wanted to be well rested.

The next morning we all met in the lobby. Wanting to arrive at Parliament Hill at approximately the same time, we left in cabs from the lobby. At Parliament Hill, we went through a security check in order to get a visitor's pass to get to the office of Pat Martin, who was the NDP representative for Winnipeg Centre.

Once inside Parliament Hill, everything was within walking distance. Everywhere we went, we went as a group. Pat Martin graciously allowed the Steelworkers use of a spare office for their headquarters during the two-week campaign/lobby. From this office, another security check was needed to get to Centre Block. All lobbyists were required to report to there. At this location, reporters, both media and print, had the opportunity to interview lobbyists.

Lawrence was our main spokesperson at this point and the interview went as planned. After the media interview, we decided to go back to headquarters. Next on our agenda was to get the MPs to support Bill C-259.

Back at the Steelworkers' borrowed headquarters, the lobby teams were phoning various MPs. The goal was to set up meetings in order to get as many MPs as possible to support the bill and have it pass. This endeavour proved time-consuming and the phone calls were not very successful.

Peter Boyle, president, United Steelworkers of America Local 343 (Kingston, Ontario,) had just arrived to join the cause. When he discovered the teams were having trouble securing meetings with MPs, he decided to try a different tactic. Once he connected with the MP's office, he informed them that he was accompanied by Vernon Theriault, and he reminded them that I was a former Westray miner. He then went on to say that I had received the Medal of Bravery for my rescue efforts at the mine, which had exploded in 1992 killing twenty-six miners.

After reciting my resumé and assuring the MPs that I was there in person, he received the sought-after meetings. I was scheduled to

The author with Peter Boyle of the Steelworkers. On the left is Del Paré of the Steelworkers.

return home after the kick-off, but because of my name being used to secure meetings, I stayed until Thursday. I couldn't stay for the duration of the campaign because of a specialist's appointment on Friday. Five years later, after two surgeries, I was still having pain in my legs and back. (In Nova Scotia, getting in to see a specialist is a long process.) After consulting with the doctor and spending some time with my family, I flew back to Ottawa on Sunday.

JUNE 2000

Upon my arrival Sunday morning (June 5), the lobby team picked me up at the airport in a van. Apparently (to cut costs) the Steelworkers rented a seven-passenger van for transporting lobbyists back and forth to Parliament Hill. Because it was Sunday, and no MPs were on the Hill, we decided to take in a local flea market. It was huge, much larger than any I had seen before. One thing I discovered about Ottawa was they did all things in a big way.

Monday was a very busy day. In the morning I was asked to tape an interview for a local cable station in Churchill, Manitoba. The late Beverly Desjarlais, then the NDP representative for that area, was the interviewer. Being interviewed for cable TV was another new experience for me, but Bev made it enjoyable.

After the interview, I was scheduled to accompany Peter Boyle and Howard Sim to meet with several MPs. The purpose of the meetings was to find out which MPs were *canaries* and which were *rats*. According to tradition, canaries were used in the mines to make sure the air was safe. Some unscrupulous companies gave workers rats instead. Rats weren't nearly as effective, but they were cheaper. Thus, MPs for Bill C-259 were *canaries*, those against were *rats*.

We set up a chart with all the MPs' names. If they were for the bill, they got a picture of a canary, if against, a picture of a rat. Thankfully, there were more canaries than rats on our chart. We were relentless in our quest to get all canaries and no rats. Some MPs could only meet with us for three to five minutes, but that was all we needed to get our message out there. Every time we went to any

Name Peter & Margarit	Party	Meeting	Date	Time	Comments	No.	Yes!
John Findlay	L	C. Block Gov Lobby	Tuesday Apr. 20	11 Am			
Stan Keyes	L	C. Block entrance	Monday Apr. 19	3:30 pm			✓?
Janko Peric	L		Tues Apr. 20	10 Am			✓
Philip Mayfield	CA	West Block 352	Apr. 29	11:45 Am			✓
Diane Marleau	L	Confederation 525	Wed May 1	3:30 pm			✓
Bob Mills	CA	Con. Lobby	Tues May 2	1 pm			✓
Ivan Grose	L	C 313	Tues Apr. 30	1:30 pm			✓✓
John Richardson	L	Justice R 100	May 3	9:30 Am			
Dave Chatters	CA	Justice 611	May 1	8:30 am		RAT	
Bob Kilger	L	members lobby	May 2	10:30 Am			✓✓
Larry McCormick	L	Conf 334	May 1	4 pm			✓✓
Rick Casson	CA	Justice 504	May 7	10:00 Am			
Rob Wood	L	East Block 309	May 7	9:15 Am			
Paul Szabo	L	Members Lobby	May 6	11:30 Am			
Joe Jordan	L						
Art Hanger	CA						

The chart used to track MPs and their position on the Westray Bill.

of the buildings on Parliament Hill we had to be checked in by the guards even though we had badges.

During the second week of lobbying, a special meeting of the Justice Committee took place, the primary focus being Bill C-259. The committee heard testimony from me and Howard Sim. Also in attendance were Lawrence McBrearty, Dennis Deveau, and David Doorey, who was the legal representative for the Steelworkers Union. Peter MacKay and Alexa McDonough both gave presentations during this session. The committee ruled unanimously to pass Bill C-259 to the next step, which was the Committee on Justice and Rights.

My testimony was basically about what it was like to work in the mine before the explosion occurred. I tried, as best as I could, to detail all the unsafe working conditions that I had personally seen. Towards the end of my testimony, I touched on my role as part of the rescue effort and how the whole experience impacted my and many other families' lives forever.

Steelworkers OnThe Hill
Ottawa June 2000

The United Steelworkers lobby groups were from around Canada, top row from left: Lawrence Hay (ON), Nancy Hutchison (ON), Cynthia Nigleki (ON), Howard Sims (NS), Vernon Theriault (NS). Bottom row: Dennis Deveau (ON), Alain Gilbert (QC), Peter Boyle (ON), Serge Mercier (QC), Del Paré (BC), National Director Lawrence McBrearty (ON), Tony McArthur (NS), Valerie Bird (ON), and Les Ellsworth (MB).

OCTOBER 2000

After the two weeks of lobbying and the many hours put in by the Steelworkers and various Members of Parliament, the prime minister called for an election. *Damn!* The Westray Bill would have to be started all over again. In Canada, once an election is called, all pending bills in the house are thrown out and have to be re-submitted. (Back to square one for us.)

There were many more people that worked tirelessly behind the scenes on that first push. Pictured above are just a few of the many lobbyists. Thank you, brothers and sisters; don't ever doubt that your work wasn't noticed and greatly appreciated.

CHAPTER 11

LOBBYING THE LAWMAKERS

SEPTEMBER 19, 2000

SEVERAL INJURIES LATER, DURING MY EMPLOYMENT AT THE FORMER Trenton Works, my back and leg pain was excruciating. The previous two back surgeries had proved ineffective. Dr. Robert Macneill, a local pain management specialist, tried facet joint injections (cortisone). Two attempts were made with the injection and both were unsuccessful. Out of treatments for my chronic pain, Dr. Macneill then referred me to Dr. Ivar Mendez in Halifax.

Dr. Mendez was, at that time, head of the neurosurgery division at Dalhousie University. After reviewing my medical history, he decided I was a good candidate for a dorsal column stimulator implant. This was not an easy process; my records and I had to be reviewed by two other specialists and Dr. Mendez. The other two doctors were a pain specialist and a psychiatrist.

All were in agreement that in my case the surgery was the next step to assist in pain management. The surgery was performed on September 19, 2000. In 2000, this procedure required a hospitalization time of five days. Today it's considered a day surgery—in and out the same day. The implant helped some, but wasn't a cure. I returned to work on October 17.

OCTOBER 10, 2000

A USWA National Health, Safety and Environment Conference was scheduled for October 11-14, 2000. My presence was requested. I flew out of Halifax on October 10 to the conference location, which was Surrey, British Columbia. Once again, I relayed my Westray experience. Every time I tell my story the load lightens a little—a form of therapy. I thank the USWA for giving me the forum to tell my story. My hope is that the more people hear it, the less chance that another "Westray" will happen.

The last day of the conference, several of us decided to play tourist and go on a "road trip." Vancouver was a bus ride away from Surrey and we all wanted to go up Grouse Mountain, the peak of Vancouver. The vehicle to get up the side of the mountain was called a "Skyride" and for me it was another once-in-a-lifetime experience. At the top of the mountain were various tourist attractions, including a restaurant. We ate at the restaurant and visited the attractions. All in all, it took the entire day and we arrived back at the hotel tired but happy that we had taken the side trip. We looked forward to returning home the next day.

FEBRUARY 26, 2001

In Ottawa, Beverly Desjarlais (NDP) had introduced private member's Bill C-284 to amend the *Criminal Code* to address corporate manslaughter. The fight was on again, just with a different bill number. C-284 had been debated in the House of Commons on September 20 and again on November 8. Because of the language, concerns were raised about unintended constitutional and Charter issues. The USWA (with the assistance of a senior criminal lawyer) provided a draft bill that addressed said issues to the Justice Committee.

MARCH 2001

A journalist with *Our Times* (called Canada's Independent Labour Magazine), Tracy Morey, wrote a front-page story for the magazine. Howard Sims and I were featured on the cover sitting in front of the Westray monument. The monument has all twenty-six miners' names and ages etched on it and is located at the Westray Memorial Park, New Glasgow: *Their light shall always shine.*

The article was entitled "The Fight of Our Lives; Making Corporate Killing A Crime," and was published in the April/May, 2001 edition. The article gives the Westray explosion background, as well as details of the lobby effort and several one-on-one interviews.

APRIL 2001

When the prime minister, Jean Chretien, called for an election in October 2000, Parliament was dissolved, thus ending proceedings that had not been completed. One such proceeding was the Westray Bill. The USWA was gathering together for another round of lobbying at Parliament Hill, and requested my presence and support. The

The sign at the Westray Memorial Park.

plan was to start lobbying on the tenth anniversary of the Westray explosion because it would be at the forefront of peoples' minds.

FEBRUARY 2002

On February 19, 2002, the House of Commons unanimously referred the matter back to the Justice Committee. Bill C-284 was withdrawn and the next steps to address corporate manslaughter were referred back to the Justice Committee.

APRIL 2002

Although Beverly Desjarlais had re-introduced "The Westray Bill," a deal was struck between the Steelworkers' lawyers and the Chretien Liberal government. It was not common knowledge, but Chretien was stepping down from the Liberal leadership and Paul Martin was replacing him. This bill was meant to be part of Chretien's legacy to Canada. The NDP withdrew the bill and the Liberal government introduced it as a "private member's bill."

The expected call from the USWA came—we were going to Parliament Hill. The tenth anniversary of the May 9, 1992, Westray explosion was coming up fast. On April 28, 2002, I flew out of Halifax headed to Ottawa. This time I was staying for the duration; I wanted this bill passed. It had been ten long years and the time had come for corporations to be held responsible for allowing employees to work unsafely.

Different hotel and different roommate. No van convoy needed; we were within walking distance to Parliament Hill. Even the ID passes to Parliament Hill were different. We had one ID pass that allowed us to go anywhere within "the Hill."

Bright and early Monday morning we began lobbying the MPs. Meeting with the various MPs was easier because of the new IDs. Some of the lobbyists were new faces, but the majority were the same group from 2000.

One meeting that stands out for me during this lobbying was with the Right Honourable Herb Gray, then second-in-command to Jean Chretien. Our group requested a five-minute meeting, which was granted. The meeting ended up lasting approximately thirty minutes. During this meeting I spoke directly with Mr. Gray regarding Westray and what I had experienced during my employment there. It seemed to me that he was very knowledgeable about Westray, which made the conversation flow easily.

APRIL 29, 2002

Monday afternoon, during a break in lobbying, I called home to let my family know how things were going. Marilyn informed me that she had received a call from the federal Standing Committee on Justice and Human Rights. The committee was requesting my presence in Ottawa to appear at a hearing as a witness. Imagine their surprise to be told that I was already in Ottawa as part of the USWA lobbyist group.

Wanting to be sure the call was legitimate, I called Peter MacKay's Ottawa office. The request was real and I was being called as a witness at the Standing Committee on Justice and Human Rights. I was scheduled to appear on May 2, 2002 from 11:00 A.M. until approximately 12:30 P.M.

MAY 2, 2002

The committee meeting that I testifying at was on a Thursday. Once again, I reported my Westray experience. I also zeroed in on the unsafe working conditions at the mine. Another part of my testimony was the fact that, after a couple of months at the mine, I had tried unsuccessfully to get my old job back at the tire shop. I told the committee that the reason I continued working at the mine was to support my family. Besides my wife, I had three small children ranging in ages from two to eight.

After my testimony was taken and entered into the record, the committee asked me several questions regarding my duties and observations at the mine. I answered to the best of my ability and my part of the meeting was completed in the allotted time frame.

At this point, it was decided that the meeting would break for lunch. My testimony being over, I approached the chairman of the committee, Andy Scott, and thanked him for requesting my presence at the committee meeting. His response was that it would soon be over.

MAY 3, 2002

On Friday all the lobbyists in attendance were invited to lunch with the MPs. This was a big deal. As a rule, only MPs ate at this location; outsiders were by invitation only. Because it was so exclusive there was a dress code. Not expecting to attend such a luncheon, I didn't have the required clothing and had to borrow a sports coat from Peter Boyle. Never having been to such a fancy lunch, I was amazed at how much silverware was at each place setting. The food was delicious, but I was glad I wasn't washing the dishes.

The luncheon was the highlight of the week, but I was glad to see the weekend come. There was another week of lobbying ahead, and I needed a break from talking about Westray.

MAY 5, 2002

All the lobbyists in attendance decided to get together for a potluck supper, and to watch the Westray documentary [A National Film Board of Canada production in 2001.] The supper was meant to both relax and rev us up for our last week of lobbying this time around.

MAY 6, 2002

Upon arrival at the lobbying office on Monday morning, I was informed that I was scheduled for a TV interview. The program was titled *Talk Politics* and was hosted by Ken Rockburn. The station I was appearing on was the commercial-free Canadian political station CPAC, or the Cable Public Affairs Channel. It was just like you see on TV—makeup was applied and I was fitted with a microphone before my appearance. I was extremely nervous, but Ken put me at ease quickly.

Like many times before, I was asked about Westray. Ken expertly guided me along the path—from the explosion to the rescue effort, then the aftermath, and the reason for lobbying on Parliament Hill. The interview lasted approximately half an hour and was aired for the first time shortly after my arrival home from lobbying.

MAY 9, 2002

It was the day of the tenth anniversary of the Westray explosion. As a tribute to the twenty-six lives lost, twenty-six miners' hats were placed around the Centennial Flame on Parliament Hill. The placing-of-the-hats ceremony was held in the morning. Immediately after the hat-placing ceremony, the USWA held a memorial service in front of the flame. Lawrence McBrearty, then president USWA (Canada) recited the names and ages of the twenty-six lost miners as listed below in alphabetical order:

John Thomas Bates, 56
Larry Arthur Bell, 25
Bennie Joseph Benoit, 42
Wayne Michael Conway, 38
Ferris Todd Dewan, 35
Adonis Joseph Dollimont, 36
Robert (Robbie) Steven Doyle, 22
Rémi Joseph Drolet, 38
Roy Edward Feltmate, 33
Charles Robert Fraser, 29
Myles Daniel Gillis, 32
John Phillip Halloran, 33
Randolph Brian House, 27
Trevor Martin Jahn, 36
Laurence Elwyn James, 34
Eugene William Johnson, 33
Stephen Paul Lilley, 40
Michael Frederick MacKay, 38
Angus Joseph MacNeil, 39
Glenn David Martin, 35

Harry Alliston McCallum, 41
Eric Earl McIsaac, 38
George James Munroe, 38
Danny James Poplar, 39
Romeo Andrew Short, 35
Peter Francis Vickers, 38.

As the names were being called out, I was reminded of how close I was to being one of them. I recalled that I had worked the overtime shift the night before, and was scheduled for my regular shift first thing the next morning. The service just strengthened my resolve to get this bill passed into law.

When the memorial service was complete, Lawrence and I were invited guests in the House of Commons. We were honoured and introduced to the Speaker by Wendy Lill, the NDP MP for Dartmouth. Being a guest in the House of Commons was a big deal and another experience I will never forget.

Peter MacKay addressed the House and spoke of the Westray mine explosion that had occurred ten years earlier. His address also touched on the bill we (the USWA and myself) were currently lobbying for.

The author with Lawrence McBrearty at a Westray memorial event in 2017.

Next to address the House was Geoff Regan, the Liberal MP for Halifax West, who spoke of the history of mining in Nova Scotia, the numerous lost lives, and the impact to the families who lost loved ones due to mining fatalities.

After MacKay and Regan spoke, the Speaker of the House requested, in honour of the tenth anniversary of the Westray disaster, that the house stand for a moment of silence, which, without question, everyone did with heads bowed in respect.

The USWA sponsored a Two Planks and a Passion Theatre production entitled *Westray—The Long Way Home,* which was a play being shown at the Arts Court Theatre in Ottawa. All the lobbyists in attendance were invited to see a showing that night. I thoroughly enjoyed the play, thought it was well written, and had the pleasure of meeting the actors afterwards. [The theatre company is from rural Kings County, Nova Scotia.]

This was my second time lobbying for the same bill (only a different official name now). During the first round of lobbying I had a break of three days in the middle. This time I was there for the duration (weekend included). It was somewhat nostalgic (being the tenth anniversary), but more intense than last time. To me, it seemed like I'd talked more about Westray in those last two weeks than I had in the last ten years.

Although it was a repeat of the first time lobbying, there was still testifying before the Committee on Justice and Human Rights, and being interviewed on a TV show. Keeping count, we'd been lobbying for this bill for four weeks out of a two-year period. It was ten years later, but reliving the Westray explosion non-stop for a solid two weeks was difficult, and I needed to get home, back to everyday life, my family, and to try to put Westray in the back of my mind. I had also been living with chronic lower back pain since 1993, and my legs and back were hurting terribly.

CHAPTER 12

LEARNING THE ROPES IN OTTAWA

APRIL 2003

EIGHT MONTHS HAD PASSED SINCE THE SECOND ROUND OF LOBBY-ing on Parliament Hill. The USWA again contacted me in hopes of enlisting my help for yet another round. This time the agenda called for three weeks of lobbying and included the House of Commons and the Senate. Wanting to help, but also taking my health into consideration, I requested a short break (weekend) either after the first or second week of lobbying.

JUNE 2003

Unbeknownst to me, the "private member's bill" had now morphed into Bill C-45. Not knowing how politics work, I didn't know that the bill had a name change. Not that it mattered to me—all I wanted was for it to be passed and into law.

October 19, 2003

Once again I flew from Halifax into Ottawa. Imagine my surprise, once I was settled in my hotel room, when I discovered there were only four of us lobbying. The lobbyists were me, Peter Boyle, Del Paré, and Dennis Deveau. First thing Monday morning, Del and I (Peter was arriving later that day) met at Dennis's office. Dennis was located locally, and from there we went to the office of NDP MP Yvon Godin. [Godin represented the New Brunswick riding of Acadie-Bathurst, and previously was a labour representative for the United Steelworkers.]

While we were in Dennis's office we strategized (because there were so few of us) on how best to use our resources. Our bill was still with the Justice and Human Rights Committee and was on its third reading. After a successful third reading (voted on and approved) the bill is then sent to the House of Commons. Once the bill is in the House of Commons, it is voted on by the MPs (needs majority approval) then passed to the Senate. Once in the Senate, the process starts again (first reading, etc). The Senate is the last step for a bill to be made into law (royal assent) or not.

After the meeting adjourned, Del and I went to the USWA's office (downtown location). We needed a copy of the names of the current members of the Senate. We were hopeful that our previous and present lobbying of the MPs would get the majority vote, and our bill would be passed to the Senate. We decided to split the senators among our small group. I would take the Maritime provinces, Del got the Western provinces, which left Ontario for Peter when he arrived.

Curious as to how the bill was going, I decided to attend the committee meeting. After the second day (Tuesday, October 21) I met with the Honourable Andy Scott (the Liberal chair of the committee) who assured me the committee meeting would be adjourned by the next day. Upon hearing this, I informed him I would see him there.

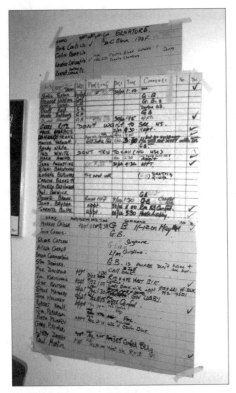

The list that the Steelworkers' lobbyists kept of senators.

Bright and early the next morning, I was at the committee meeting anxiously awaiting the bill to be passed to the House of Commons. It seemed to take an eternity, but finally, it happened. I was elated—the Justice and Human Rights Committee did the right thing (as far as USWA and I were concerned) for blue-collar workers.

Now the lobbying began in earnest. With the bill being passed to the House of Commons, the next step was for the bill to be passed from the House to the Senate. We needed the majority of the MPs to approve the bill.

One of our best avenues to attain meetings (however short) with MPs was Question Period. In Canada, Question Period is when MPs discuss and debate bills before voting on whether to send said bill onto the Senate. Because Question Period has all MPs together in one place, access (by us) was important for lobbying purposes. Our passes allowed us to attend Question Period and we were there regularly until the vote was cast. During the breaks was when the most lobbying took place. I talked and ate with enough politicians then to last me a lifetime.

I was informed by Dennis that it would take several days for our bill to come from the Justice Committee to the House of Commons. I had packed a tape recorder on this trip and decided to take advantage of some free time and record my Westray experience. Because it was an integral part, I also recorded my personal life happenings in the same timeline.

OCTOBER 27, 2003

Monday was a wash. We waited patiently at the House of Commons all day while the MPs had the third reading of Bill C-45. Finally in the early evening the vote was taken. The bill successfully passed the House, and was now on its way to the Senate.

In the event that the bill passed to the Senate, I had set up meetings with various senators for Tuesday morning. One such meeting was with the Honourable Michael Forrestall who was from Dartmouth, Nova Scotia. The meeting was scheduled to take place in his Ottawa office. While waiting for the meeting to take place, I struck up a conversation with Senator Forrestall's legal advisor Joseph Varner—he was married to a New Glasgow native, Lisa, and through my hockey activities. I was acquainted with her father, Dan MacLeod.

The author with Senator Mike Forrestall.

During this conversation, the senator entered the room and the meeting began. First on the agenda was to get his support for the Westray Bill. During our discussion soliciting his support of Bill C-45, Senator Forrestall shared a personal story with us. I was confused, the story (to me) had nothing to do with the Westray Bill, and shortly afterward our meeting time was up. Upon leaving his office, I was under the impression that we didn't have his support. Hoping to get another chance to change the senator's mind, I left my cellphone number with the receptionist.

OCTOBER 29, 2003

Bright and early Wednesday morning (9 A.M.) our group of three was scheduled to attend an Atlantic Liberal caucus meeting. The meeting was arranged by Senator Wilfred Moore, from Nova Scotia. Also attending were the other Liberal senators and the Members of Parliament from the Atlantic region. Our objective was to get the party's support for Bill C-45.

Not knowing that you are supposed to turn off your phone during meetings, I had left mine on. During the meeting when my phone rang, I excused myself and stepped out into the hallway to take the call. Only select people had the number for my phone, so I knew the call was important. The call was from Conservative Senator Mike Forrestall's office requesting another meeting with us that day. I explained that we were presently in a meeting with the Liberal senators and MPs. Our plan (after the meeting) was to go to the Centre Block and lobby some more. Because of the call, I told his office we would change our plans and drop by after our meeting if that was acceptable.

Forrestall invited us into his office and proceeded to inform us that he was in favour of Bill C-45. He also told us of his intentions to debate the bill that day in the Senate. In this session, the Senate sat on Tuesday, Wednesday, and Thursday beginning at 2 P.M. Senator Forrestall graciously invited us to attend the sitting, and we quickly accepted.

Peter Boyle had packed bright yellow USWA T-shirts in his luggage. Wanting to stand out in the Senate gallery, we decided to wear them. Not knowing when Bill C-45 would be brought up for debate, we sat patiently waiting in the gallery. As promised, towards the end of Wednesday's session, Senator Forrestall began the debate of Bill C-45 (the Westray Bill).

After a brief history of the bill's journey from C-284 to C-45 the first reading had begun. Senator Forrestall recited the history of Westray, acknowledged our presence in the gallery, and urged for an expeditious dealing with Bill C-45. He acknowledged the shortfalls, confirmed his support, then read Bill C-45 in its entirety.

When Senator Forrestall finished, the Honourable John G. Bryden (a bill C-45 supporter) spoke. Senator Bryden gave a brief history of his association with the mining industry (as a USWA lawyer), his support of the bill, and then he requested that the bill be a priority. The senator wanted the bill sent to the Standing Senate Committee on Legal and Constitutional Affairs. He was concerned about significant clauses and wanted to be sure the bill did what it purported to do.

Senator Moore (a Bill C-45 supporter) addressed the House and requested that (with opposition agreement) the bill be read for the third time now. Senator Bryden said that he wanted the bill to go through the normal procedure, which meant that it be sent to committee and approved before third reading.

The Honourable Noël A. Kinsella (deputy leader of the Opposition) then spoke and stated that the Official Opposition in the Senate supported the adoption of the bill in the most expeditious of ways possible. The hope was that the bill would go to the Standing Senate Committee on Legal and Constitutional Affairs, which sat at 10:45 A.M. the next morning.

The Honourable Sharon Carstairs, leader of the government in the Senate, then spoke. She affirmed her support of Bill C-45 and also requested it be sent to committee for the following morning.

Next up was the Honourable Dan Hays, Senate Speaker. Basically what happened was the motion (for second reading) was moved by Senator Moore and seconded by Senator Rose-Marie Losier-Cool. The motion passed and the bill was referred to committee. Only one more reading to go after the bill returned from committee.

OCTOBER 30, 2003

Next morning the four of us attended the Standing Senate Committee on Legal and Constitutional Affairs. Nine senators, two members of the Standing Committee on Justice and Human Rights, and a clerk made up the committee. The meeting was approximately an hour long. Attending the proceedings was a once-in-a-lifetime occurrence—history was being made right before my eyes. Bill C-45 was approved by the committee, and sent back to Senate for afternoon session.

Peter, Del, Dennis, and I had a couple of hours before the Senate sat, so we decided to get some lunch. Our main discussion during lunch was how fast the bill went from Senate to committee and back to Senate. Not knowing how long we would be in the Senate Gallery, we prepared ourselves for a long afternoon.

Rather than starting at the usual time (2 P.M.) Senate started at 1:30 P.M. Bill C-45 (Bill to Amend the *Criminal Code*) was addressed first. The Honourable George J. Furey, chair of the Standing Senate Committee on Legal and Constitutional Affairs, presented his eighth report. After that, the Speaker asked assembled senators when the bill would be read a third time. Senator Moore motioned that the bill be placed on the Orders of the Day for third reading later in the day. Motion passed.

Towards the end of session, our moment finally arrived. Senator Moore moved for the third reading of Bill C-45, to amend the *Criminal Code* (criminal liability of organizations).

Senators Moore, Andreychuk, Kinsella, Robichaud, Lynch-Staunton, all debated Bill C-45 until 6 P.M. The Speaker interrupted with a request that the senators all agree not to see the clock. All senators agreed and the discussion continued. Eventually Senator

Carstairs, after meeting with committee, put their request forward that the bill be given a formal royal assent. The senators agreed to adopt the motion; the bill was read the third time and passed.

Forgetting the setting which we were in, our group stood and began clapping. The Senate guard was dispatched to remind us where we were and to remain quiet during the proceedings. After the session was adjourned, our group assembled in the hallway to express our thanks to the various senators who had supported Bill C-45.

It seemed like it took an eternity—ten years—but finally the fight was over with a win for our side. Royal assent (when the bill is written into law) was Friday, November 7, 2003, only a week away. Before I had agreed to come for this round of lobbying, I had requested a weekend back home in the middle. Thinking this was the perfect time for a couple of days home, I asked when my flight was departing. Imagine my surprise when I was told I wasn't returning home for the weekend. And to top it off, no explanation was given why. Angry and disappointed, I had to phone home and say I wasn't coming home until the next week after royal assent was complete.

Meanwhile, Peter Boyle, who resided in Kingston (two hours away) was making arrangements to return home. Apparently an Eastern Ontario Council meeting was scheduled for Saturday with Local 343 (Kingston) hosting. Peter graciously offered to take Del and me to Kingston with him. To make the offer more attractive, he offered us a tour of Kingston as well as all expenses paid by his local. Not wanting to spend another weekend in Ottawa, and with no prospect of going home, Del and I accepted his offer.

October 31, 2003

Early Friday morning the three of us left Ottawa in Peter's vehicle. The two-hour drive took longer because Peter was reciting the history and showing us the sights as we drove.

One of the sights was the location of the first Government House of Commons (now the home of Kingston City Hall). Although we didn't see the exact house (protected from public viewing) we were a stone's throw away. The original House overlooks Lake Ontario and approximately ten minutes down the same road we arrived at the front doors of the Kingston Penitentiary. Next we visited Grant Hall, a landmark located on the Queen's University campus. Tired from driving and sightseeing, we checked into our hotel, ate, and packed it in for the night.

November 1, 2003

The next day (Saturday) Peter retrieved us from the hotel and we headed to the union meeting. At the meeting, we discussed our Parliament Hill and lobbying experience. We also stressed the importance of the USWA working together. Towards the end of the meeting there was a "Q & A" session focused on Bill C-45's progression from start to law. Afterwards everyone posed for pictures and general talk.

Also, after the meeting I was presented with an "Eyes on Lives" poster-sized plaque. On the reverse were USWA signatures and personal comments. The presentation brought tears to my eyes and appreciation to the brotherhood for standing together for such a worthy cause.

As the weekend drew to a close, we went to Peter's residence. It was a nice fall day so we decided to go to Peter's cabin on the lake. The cabin was in a beautiful spot, approximately thirty minutes away from his residence going towards Ottawa. We were at the cabin until early evening, then returned back to Ottawa for royal assent week. The weekend away was just what I needed to prepare for the last week of my Ottawa experience. The bill that I had the privilege of being such a big part of was finally being put into law.

The usual procedure for royal assent is the bill is sent over to Government House for the governor general of Canada to sign. At that time the governor general was Adrienne Clarkson.

Dennis Deveau (Steelworkers' representative, Ottawa) requested from the Liberals a special procedure. His thought was that because it was a long battle fought by workers for workers across Canada, the signing should be commemorated in a more public display.

The special procedure requested was a ceremonial royal assent. Basically what happens in ceremonial royal assent is that the governor general of Canada assumes a throne in the Senate. Members of the House of Commons (senators along with the speaker) march to the senate and present the passed bill to the governor general for signing. After the bill is signed by the governor general, it becomes law.

CHAPTER 13

THE BIG DAY

NOVEMBER 3, 2003

THE BEGINNING OF OUR LAST WEEK IN OTTAWA WAS UPON US. THIS week was unlike any of the others because on Friday we would see all our hard work reach fruition. Most of the week was uneventful in that we were just killing time. Peter returned home for a couple of days (returned Thursday). Del and I spent our downtime by going to various MP offices thanking them for their support, attending some Question Period sessions, and generally hanging around the temporary headquarters supplied for us.

NOVEMBER 6, 2003

The USWA invited Allen and Debbie Martin (all expenses paid) to attend the royal assent. Allen and Debbie were two of several of the spokespeople for Westray families. They were also members of the Westray Memorial Board and had lost a close family member at Westray, Allen's brother Glenn Martin. They arrived in Ottawa

The author outside Rideau Hall, home of the governor general.

Thursday morning, with the royal assent being held early the next day. Peter also arrived in Ottawa around the same time.

Shortly after Allen, Debbie, and Peter's arrival, we gathered at Parliament Hill. It had been arranged for us to have pictures taken with Prime Minister Jean Chretien. Whenever the prime minister of Canada made an appearance on the Hill, multiple people/groups requested photos with him. While waiting for our turn for photos we were told that senators were there for photos as well. Being a big hockey fan, imagine my surprise when I discovered the senators were not from the House of Commons but some of the members of the Ottawa Senators hockey team.

Not one to miss an opportunity, I asked to have my picture taken with the players as well as the prime minister. The NHL players who agreed to photos were Jason Spezza, Chris Phillips, and Wade Redden. As well as posing for pictures, the athletes gave me

The author with Right Honourable Jean Chretien.

autographs. Shortly after the pictures were taken with the hockey players, it was our turn for pictures with the prime minister. A group photo was taken, then I also got an individual picture with just the prime minister and me.

I'm not sure which was the bigger deal to me, pictures with the hockey players or an individual picture with Jean Chretien. After the photo session was complete, I asked the prime minister if he would personally sign a letter that I had received from him back in November 1994 and he cheerfully complied.

November 7, 2003

The big day had finally arrived—history was being made in Canada. Peter, Del, Allen, Debbie, union representative Mike Piche, and I met for breakfast before heading over to the Hill. There were so many people involved in helping to make this happen that I couldn't begin to

The author outside Chretien's office.

list them all. I would like to take this opportunity to thank each and every one of them for their help whether it was a small or a large part. Without them, this bill would never have happened.

After breakfast, as a group, we headed to the Hill. When we arrived at the Senate where the royal assent was to take place, there was a lot of activity. Because the area was filling up quickly, we decided to take our seats and wait for the proceedings to begin.

Never having witnessed anything like this before, I was excited. At the beginning of the session the Senate Speaker welcomes everyone, then exits the chair. Next the Senate is adjourned by the arrival of Her Excellency, the governor general of Canada. The governor general is then seated in the vacant Speaker's chair (now the throne) and the House of Commons is summoned.

The House of Commons consists of the Members of Parliament and they are not present when the governor general is seated, thus the summons. Our group had a front row seat in the gallery for this series of events. The members from the House of Commons are then summoned by the Usher of the Black Rod who escorts the MPs down the hall from the House to the Senate to witness the bill being passed into law. It seemed to me after the escorted arrival of the MPs the room was crowded. Once the bill was signed by the governor general, our group was invited to the chambers of the Speaker of the Senate. Lunch was provided for the guests in chambers as well as photos with Her Excellency the governor general of Canada.

The luncheon was a low-key affair, but for me, a major accomplishment. The Westray journey had begun for me in 1992. Now it was 2003 and successfully completed. All that had happened in between I will never forget; it was a once-in-a-lifetime experience and I had learned a lot. After the luncheon, I took the opportunity to shake hands and thank the individuals in attendance for their contributions to the successful passing of Bill C-45. Knowing the chances of ever seeing some of these people again, I thought it was important that they know their efforts were appreciated, and it was a pleasure for me to meet each and every one of them.

During my stay in Ottawa, everywhere I went I had my Medal of Bravery pinned to my chest. Up until that moment, the medal didn't have any special meaning to me, but after this journey, I realized its importance. Looking forward to going home, that evening was a quiet one. I relayed, into my tape recorder, the events preceding, during, and after this historic day while still fresh in my mind.

November 8, 2003

Bright and early Saturday morning, I was heading to the airport for the trip back home. The ten-year journey for Bill C-45 to be made into law was finally over. I am proud that I could play a significant role in this law coming into effect. The law now states:

> Organizations are now considered criminally liable for the actions of senior members and anyone who directs work is legally bound to take reasonable measures to protect employees' safety.

> My hope now is that this law may never have to be enforced.

WHAT WAS THE WESTRAY BILL (BILL C-45)?

The Westray Bill or Bill C-45 was federal legislation that amended the Canadian *Criminal Code* and became law on March 31, 2004. The Bill (introduced in 2003) established new legal duties for workplace health and safety and imposed serious penalties for violations that result in injuries or death. The Bill provided new rules for attributing criminal liability to organizations, including corporations, their representatives, and those who direct the work of others.

NOTE: The Canadian federal government reuses bill numbers. Currently Bill C-45 is being used to announce Act(s) respecting cannabis and to amend the *Controlled Drugs and Substances Act*, the *Criminal Code,* and other Acts.

SECTIONS OF THE CRIMINAL CODE

The amendment added Section 217.1 to the *Criminal Code* which reads:

> "**217.1** Every one who undertakes, or has the authority, to direct how another person does work or performs a task is under a legal duty to take reasonable steps to prevent bodily harm to that person, or any other person, arising from that work or task."

The amendment also added Sections 22.1 and 22.2 to the *Criminal Code* imposing criminal liability on organizations and its representatives for negligence (22.1) and other offences (22.2).

SOURCE:
Fact Sheet on Bill C-45. http://www.ccohs.ca/oshanswers/legisl/billc45. html. Canadian Centre for Occupational Health and Safety website. Reproduced with the permission of CCOHS, 2017.

CHAPTER 14

SPREADING THE MESSAGE

"There is no question that management knew that the levels of methane underground at Westray were hazardous. Management was aware, or ought to have been aware, that, under section 72 of the Coal Mines Regulation Act, such conditions mandated the withdrawal of workers from the affected areas."

—THE WESTRAY REPORT

NOVEMBER 22, 2003

APPROXIMATELY TWO WEEKS AFTER I RETURNED FROM OTTAWA, I was interviewed by my local newspaper. The interview was titled "Bill C-45: A Long Time Coming." The focus was my experiences in the process of getting Bill C-45 into law. From lobbying with the USWA,

Ken Neumann, standing, and Lawrence McBrearty.

getting support for the bill from the MPs on Parliament Hill, then getting support from the Senate to pass the bill into law.

I was also asked (during the interview) what it felt like to witness (and be a big part of) history being made. Another question was what happens with the bill (now law) now? My answer to the "what happens now?" question was that workers/employees had to be educated as to what their rights under this law are. The answer to the first question was that although it took a huge emotional toll on myself and my family, it is an experience I will never forget.

JANUARY, APRIL 2004

Several months after the interview, I was again contacted by the USWA. They requested my presence (all expenses paid) to speak at the National Policy Conference. This year it was being held in Vancouver from April 21 to 24, 2004. Of course I accepted, and on April 20 found myself yet again flying to Vancouver.

I arrived in Vancouver early in the afternoon (I always choose a morning flight). Upon arrival, I went directly to the hotel where the conference was being held and I was staying to register. That evening there was a hospitality suite at the hotel sponsored by the Steelworkers, which I attended, before the start of business the next day. The agenda for the conference was well planned, and I knew it would be a busy three days.

According to the agenda, I wasn't scheduled to speak until Friday—the last day was Saturday—so I attended as many of the meetings as I could squeeze into that short period of time. When it was my turn to speak, I opened with a heartfelt thank you to the Steelworkers for all their combined efforts in making Bill C-45 into law. I singled out Lawrence McBrearty thanking him for his leadership on Parliament Hill. Lawrence at that time was stepping down as national director of the USWA and was handing over the reins to Ken Neumann.

I chose not to speak about the Westray mine itself, but instead what brought me from a small town in Pictou County, Nova Scotia,

The author in the Pittsburgh office of Leo Gerard of the USWA.

to lobbying in Ottawa on Parliament Hill for a bill that eventually became law after a four-year battle. My first policy conference with the Steelworkers had been in 1999, and that was when I was singled out as a Westray survivor. The main point of my speech was to let the assembled Steelworkers know that by working together (and not giving up) there was a light at the end of the tunnel.

On a personal note, I wanted to thank the Steelworkers and supporters of Bill C-45 for encouraging me to speak out, giving me a chance to tell my story, and allowing me to be a part of making history. I ended my speech with this message:

> Encourage your members to become active in their union by giving them the opportunities that the USWA gave to me. Many thanks to all of you, and remember: *NO MORE WESTRAYS.*

May 2004

The timing of the conference worked out perfectly. I arrived back home in time for the annual Westray miners' remembrance. Every year on May 9, family and friends of the twenty-six lost miners meet at the Memorial Park located in New Glasgow.

We Remember Westray began at 7 P.M. with prayers written by Reverend Glen Matheson. This was followed by a recounting of the events that took place on that fateful day and the days thereafter. Although it had been over ten years since the tragedy, I still found this time of year hardest. To me, it's like the disaster happened yesterday.

August 2004

USWA (Health, Safety, and Environment) were hosting another conference from August 22 to 25 in Pittsburgh, Pennsylvania. On the agenda was a Westray Success Panel Discussion. I was asked to address the members attending the conference. They wanted me to speak about working at the mine, the rescue effort, lobbying for Bill C-45, and the passing of said bill into law.

At this point in time, it felt like I was becoming a veteran air traveller. I was still having back issues and knew I could only sit for short periods of time. The airlines' flight attendants were very accommodating when I couldn't sit and allowed me to stand at the back of the plane.

After settling into my hotel, I went to Leo Gerard's (international president, USWA) office. Always looking for the opportunity of once-in-a-lifetime pictures, I got one of me sitting behind Leo's desk, with him standing close by.

While in Pittsburgh with some free time on my hands, I decided to take in a few sporting events. Upon discussion with the concierge at the hotel, I realized I couldn't afford football ($500 a pop) and settled for baseball ($9.00 to $27.00). With a more reasonable ticket price, some fellow conference goers and I attended three separate evening games (Arizona Diamondbacks vs. Pittsburgh Pirates).

During and after the conference I extended a blanket invitation to several of the attendees that if they were ever in Pictou County and wanted a guided tour of Westray to give me a call.

September 2004

Back in November of 2003 when Bill C-45 reached royal assent, I had a conversation with Senator Moore. I had requested a presentation of the official sealed copies of the changes to the *Criminal Code* of Canada as a result of the passage of Bill C-45 for my own personal records. Senator Moore agreed to put together a package of the copies I requested and mail them to me.

In early September, I received a phone call from Senator Moore's office requesting my mailing address. Not long after I received a letter from the senator and some official documents. The letter explained why I couldn't get the documents that I had requested, but the closest copies allowable at this time. The package contained three copies of Senator Moore's speech (at the third reading). Next was a copy of the sealed law with an additional twenty-six copies of the official sealed law for each of the deceased miners' families. And last, but certainly

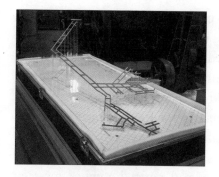

Items that were part of the Westray display at the Museum of Industry in Stellarton: a model of the mine, a hard hat, a Westray draeger breather, and a commemorative canary pin.

not least, pictures taken in chambers of the Speaker of the Senate following royal assent.

NOVEMBER 2004

In the middle of November I received a phone call from USWA—a Constitutional Convention was being scheduled for April 11 to 14, 2005, in Las Vegas, Nevada. My presence was requested as a distinguished guest and again all my expenses were paid.

Flight time was the morning of April 11 from Halifax arriving in Las Vegas in the early evening. Being from a small town in Nova Scotia, I wasn't prepared for the light show on the plane's approach to the city. I can't think of the words to describe the sights—only that it was awesome and you have to see it for yourself.

After deplaning, I proceeded to the claim check for my luggage, which, after waiting patiently for a while, did not appear. Not having had this happen before, I went to the front desk at the airport. They took my name, a description of my luggage, and the hotel where I was staying and said they would call me when the luggage appeared.

Upon arriving in my hotel room, I noticed a phone message waiting. Thinking it was the airport, I retrieved the message. Rather than being the airport, it was Peter Boyle. Apparently I and several others, including Leo Gerard, were appearing on the conference stage first thing in the morning. Once again, thank goodness Peter and I were similar in size since I had to borrow appropriate clothing from him. Thankfully, my luggage arrived at the hotel the night of my first appearance at the conference.

As a "distinguished guest," I had the perk of being able to sit on stage during the whole conference. During the conference, two unions joined together to become one—United Steel, Paper and Forestry, Rubber, Manufacturing, Energy, Allied Industrial and Service Workers International Union. The theme of the conference was "Building Power to Serve Our Members." Sitting on stage, at any given time, I would look out at the attendees and be amazed by the sheer number of people there. A year had passed since Bill C-45 became law, and we were still waiting for it to be applied.

MAY 2008

The annual Westray service was just around the corner. I received an invitation via mail to the Museum of Industry before the service. The museum was re-opening the exhibit *Coal and Grit*. The agenda included several speakers, and grade four students from A. G. Baillie Memorial School laying roses. At the end was a ribbon-cutting ceremony to open the Coal and Grit area of the museum, followed by a reception.

During the commemoration of the sixteenth anniversary, while moving through the exhibits, I was approached by a woman I didn't know. She asked if I would pose for a picture with my picture. Confused I looked through the exhibit and found a picture of myself sitting in front of the memorial at Memorial Park on display.

In the exhibit where my picture was displayed, the Westray mine disaster was in the forefront. Also included was interesting information about coal mines. After I posed for the picture, I was surprised to see towards the end of the exhibit hand-drawn pictures prominently displayed. In this display were the drawings the children had given us during the Westray rescue effort. Upon seeing these drawings again, I remembered how they had given me the strength, energy, and courage to continue. Later that evening the memorial service was held. As before it was held at Memorial Park, where we prayed and fondly remembered twenty-six miners who perished.

To my surprise and delight, a couple from Pittsburgh took me up on my invitation for a guided tour of Westray a month later. I took them to the exhibit first, then to the Westray site. The tour brought back bittersweet memories of both the trip to Pittsburgh and the Westray disaster.

PART FOUR

THE
ANNIVERSARIES

CHAPTER 15

TWENTY-YEAR ANNIVERSARY

FEBRUARY 2009

In New Glasgow, we have a group called the Pictou County Injured Workers Association. I was still having back issues at this time and battling WCB about benefits. Thinking that maybe this group might know of an avenue I had not tried, I contacted Larry Mahoney (intake worker) about my case. We scheduled a meeting, he took my information, and thus started my association with this organization. In my case, with Larry's help, an appeal was filed [to WCB] and subsequently denied. I was impressed with what the association stood for and began attending meetings every month. I did this for approximately four years and still, to this day, have frequent contact with them.

People march in New Glasgow in 2012, demanding No More Westrays.

APRIL 2011

One evening in early April, I was relaxing at home with the TV on in the background. What caught my attention was a news report about two workers being killed on separate job sites. It felt like my heart was caught in my throat. I had thought that all our hard work in getting Bill C-45 passed would help prevent this from happening.

Not knowing what else to do, and with the backing of the Pictou County Injured Workers Association, I did several newspaper interviews. Our goal was to get more workers and companies aware that Bill C-45 was now law—that workplace tragedies need not happen. Unfortunately because our group was so small, the word didn't get far enough.

FEBRUARY 2012

May 2012 would be the twentieth anniversary of the Westray disaster. In early February, the USW again made contact. Something was being planned in Ottawa—I didn't know what—to commemorate the anniversary on May 7. The USW requested that I attend and give a speech. [In 2005 the USWA became the USW.]

Not sure if I wanted to be in Ottawa so close to the anniversary, I asked if I could think about it and get back to them. I was assured I would be home in time for the local memorial service, but I still had reservations. Being away from my family so much during the process of getting Bill C-45 passed, I decided to consult them about my returning to Ottawa. It had been eight years since the Bill was passed and life (for me) had returned to reasonably normal.

After our family meeting, and with my wife's and children's blessing, it was decided I would yet again return to Ottawa. I returned the USW's phone call and accepted their invitation.

MAY 2012

On May 7, I was back in Ottawa. Pat Van Horne (USW director–Ottawa) retrieved me from the airport. I was taken to Pat's office and given a verbal agenda of what was taking place the next day on Parliament Hill. Pat informed me that the USW was taking this opportunity (the twentieth Westray anniversary) to launch an awareness campaign. It was to focus on the changes made to the *Criminal Code* with Bill C-45. My role was to talk about Westray and my role as part of the lobbying group.

Knowing I had limited time to give my speech, I put my thoughts on paper. With Pat's help, we reduced the written thoughts into a speech with all the key points covered. That evening Ken Neumann, by now national director USW, invited us to join him for supper. We went to a nice restaurant with great food and the conversation was mostly about what was to take place the next day. By the time the meal was finished, it was late. Once I returned to my hotel room, I decided to review my notes for the speech. Next thing I knew it was morning. I had fallen asleep while reviewing my notes, which were strewn around me on the hotel bed.

The plan was for Pat, Ken, and me to meet for breakfast at the hotel I was staying at. My mind whirling with the speech I was giving, I got ready and went downstairs. After breakfast, with more discussion about the day ahead, we caught a cab to Parliament Hill.

Although it had been several years since I had been there, the Centre Block's procedures hadn't changed. We went through the check area, got our passes, then onto the newsroom. They weren't quite ready for us, so we waited in another room adjacent to the newsroom. Now that the time was here, I began to get nervous about the speech I was about to give. Peter MacKay, then Defence Minister, joined us in the waiting room. Glad to see my representative and a friendly face, we engaged in generalities, which helped with the nervousness a little bit. Shortly afterward we were informed that the newsroom was ready for us.

Ken Neumann was up first reviewing the events that were taking place in Pictou County the following day, including the Westray Memorial Service. Ken then read a statement prepared by Allen Martin whose brother perished at Westray. My turn was next. Ken introduced me and I took my place behind the microphone.

I was still quite nervous and mentally telling myself, *Vernon, you can do this, keep it together and don't break down*. I was wearing the T-shirt given to me in 1999 ("Workers' Rights are Human Rights") with my Medal of Bravery pinned to my chest. Although I had my notes in front of me, I didn't need them. Once I started talking, the words came from my heart. After I finished, I wasn't feeling very good. My legs felt like rubber, and my stomach was so upset that I thought I was going to puke.

After me, Peter MacKay took the podium. Peter talked about the upcoming twentieth anniversary and answered questions from the attending reporters. Next was Labour Minister Lisa Raitt, followed by NDP MP Robert Chisholm, and closing was, again, Ken Neumann.

Shortly after the speeches were finished, Pat's cellphone began ringing. Several reporters and local TV stations wanted to interview me. They wanted to do follow-up interviews about Westray—twenty years later. I wanted to be home for the memorial service so I only had time for two on-camera interviews at local TV stations in Ottawa. True to their word, the USW got me home that night (May 8) in plenty of time for the memorial service the next day. I was accompanied on my flight home by Peter Boyle, and several USW union members.

The next morning, after I awoke in my own bed, Marilyn suggested we watch the videos on YouTube from the previous day. I hadn't seen them yet, and was anxious to see if I had gotten my message out there. The videos of the various speeches and subsequent TV interviews can be viewed on YouTube: *Westray 20th Anniversary; Vernon Theriault May 8, 2012; and Vernon Theriault on Parliament Hill.* I was quite emotional after watching the videos, so much so that they brought tears to my eyes.

There were many people in town for the twentieth anniversary memorial service. Besides the USW members who flew home with me, there were family and friends of the lost miners. After viewing the videos, I decided to go to the hotel where Peter Boyle and the majority of USW members were staying. We had coffee together and talked about the events that had occurred over the last twenty years.

The day's events began at 5:18 A.M. (the exact time of the explosion). At noon, North Nova Education Centre hosted a commemorative ceremony for the twentieth anniversary. The ceremony was

Debbie Martin, a relative of one of the Westray victims, lays flowers during the memorial event.

well attended and included the visiting members of the USW, family and friends of the fallen miners, and members of the community.

I was scheduled to give a televised interview with *Live at 5*. The interviewer was Steve Murphy (CTV News) and the program was watched province-wide with the possibility of being shown nationally.

After the ceremony (at North Nova) and before the interview there was some free time. The visiting Steelworkers and I were hungry, and not knowing when we would have the opportunity to eat a proper meal, we decided to go to an eatery close by. There were eighteen of us in total, and in a small community like Stellarton, we didn't know if we could find a place to accommodate us all. After a few phone calls we found an eatery that would be able to push tables together and had a pleasant meal. During the meal we discussed what had happened so far that day and what was to come.

Once the meal and discussion were finished, I proceeded to Memorial Park for my scheduled interview with Steve Murphy. Joining me for the interview was one of the widows of the deceased miners.

Shortly after the interview, the service began. The service was sad and heartbreaking. Among the many attendees were some of the draegermen from the 1992 explosion. Also there were several young people who weren't even born during that period, but wanted to be a part of the service.

North Nova held a reception after the service on its campus. It was a long day for me with many sad and fond memories of the last twenty years. As the events wound down and the day was coming to a close I wondered what the future would hold for us now.

The next day everybody left Pictou County and went back home. I hope that the Steelworkers keep on doing what they are good at, which is fighting for working people. Sometime during the day I had gotten a call from Ken Bingham (chief technology officer, ACM Facility Safety, located in Calgary, Alberta). Because I wasn't at home for the majority of the day I didn't know he had called until the evening. He left a message and number. [On its website,

CTV's Steve Murphy interviewing the author and Westray widow Genesta Halloran, who lost her husband, John, in the tragedy.

ACM states: "Located in Calgary, AB, ACM Facility Safety is Canada's largest independent provider of Hazard Analysis, Safeguard and Risk Assessment services."]

I decided to give Ken a call back the next day. I waited until afternoon because of the time difference. When I got Ken on the phone, he told me he had seen the twentieth-anniversary Westray interview yesterday on the news. Ken asked if I was interested in coming to Calgary for a visit (at his expense). He wanted to meet me in person and show me his company. I agreed to the meeting. This would be my first time in Calgary.

Marcel Leal-Valias was assigned the task of picking me up at the airport and taking me to Ken's office in downtown Calgary. I was introduced to the office staff, then Marcel took me to the hotel. Later that evening Ken and several of his staff members (Marcel included) picked me up at the hotel to go to eat. We went to a nice restaurant not far from the hotel. I ordered a steak but after seeing the ribs (they looked delicious) I was sorry I hadn't ordered them instead. During the meal, Ken said his company had been around a long time, and he had just recently opened a new office. He then asked if I might be interested in returning in June for the grand opening as a guest speaker. I told him I would think about it.

Shortly after we finished eating, I returned to the hotel and tried to rest. Because of the time difference it had been a long day. The next morning I walked over to the office around 9:00. Ken was already in his office and told me to make myself at home. I was then given a tour of the different safety measures the company had in place. After the tour was complete I rejoined Marcel. He said supper had been arranged at a restaurant different from the one the night before. The restaurant was called Gaucho Brazilian Barbeque. The plan was that I would be flying home later that night.

The dinner was incredible—so many unique flavours to choose from. The serving of the food was different from what I'm used to. The waiters circulated around the room with various meats. Each customer had a card in front of them. If your card was face up, you wanted some of what the waiter was offering. The card was placed face down when you had enough on your plate or didn't want any of what was being offered.

After the meal and on my way to the airport, I told Marcel I would call within the next week with my decision about June. He expressed his wish that my decision would be in the positive.

JUNE 2012

Upon returning home, I had to rest for a few days. Because of the trip to Calgary being short, my back pain was more intense than usual. After my back pain lessened (a few days), I called Ken. I gave him the good news that I would be attending the grand opening in June as a guest speaker.

Ken had scheduled me to speak on June 14 from 6:30 to 7:30 P.M. I was to talk about Bill C-45 and Westray. Organizers showed the news video from May 8, 2012, in Ottawa. In the video, I was introduced by Ken Neumann. After the video was shown, I talked to the audience about working at the mine and getting Bill C-45 passed into law. After I finished speaking, I answered questions. We broke for lunch. The buffet was a casual affair and allowed all the attendees to mingle. I realized it was getting late—my flight was leaving at 11:00 P.M. I said my good-byes and left the grand opening to prepare for my flight home.

July 2012

Life again had returned to somewhat normal. Mid-July I received a phone call from Pat Van Horne (USW). There was a symposium being held in Ottawa on October 24 and 25 at the University of Ottawa. The main purpose of the symposium was fine-tuning Bill C-45. She asked if I was willing to attend and speak at the symposium.

October 2012

Once again, I was on a plane headed to Ottawa. The symposium was called Westray +20. Upon arrival, I was shown the agenda, and was scheduled to speak towards the end of the first night at a reception. Among the attendees at the reception were professors, defence lawyers, police officers, and prosecutors. The main topic of discussion was how Bill C-45 would be applied in prosecutions. At that time, the bill had not been applied to hold employers or corporate executives liable for workplace safety or injuries.

Involved with Bill C-45 in its infancy, I was pleased with the discussions and questions posed at the two-day symposium. My role was to speak about working at Westray, how unsafe the mine was, and the aftermath of the explosion.

After speaking about the mine, I then spoke about my journey with Bill C-45 from beginning to end. On a personal note, I spoke of how the disaster affected my family and my disappointment that the bill had yet to be applied. My speech ended with my hope that the symposium was the start of educating the public and employers about Bill C-45.

CHAPTER 16

TWENTY-FIVE YEARS LATER

"Westray managers not only failed to promote and nurture any kind of safe work ethic but actually discouraged any meaningful dialogue on safety issues. Management did so through an aggressive and authoritarian attitude towards the employees, as well as the use of offensive and abusive language. Westray workers quickly came to realize that their safety concerns fell on deaf ears and that management's open-door policy was mere window dressing."
—THE WESTRAY REPORT

MARCH 2014

TWO YEARS HAD QUIETLY PASSED SINCE THE SYMPOSIUM IN OTTAWA. In early March, I received a call from the USW. Sylvia Boyce (District 6, safety, health and environment), Steve Hunt (president, District 3), and Ken Neumann (national director for Canada) were making an official visit to Pictou County. They would arrive on March 10.

First on the agenda was to lay a wreath on the Westray monument. This was accomplished on the tenth at 1:00 P.M. Afterwards I was again on the news conducting an interview about how Bill C-45, now part of the *Criminal Code* of Canada, was not being enforced.

The USW representatives had made arrangements for themselves, me, some members of the Pictou County Injured Workers Association, and members of the Westray Families Group to dine at a restaurant located in Pictou. Later that night, a public meeting was scheduled with the Pictou County Municipality. Our goal was to have as many people as possible become knowledgeable about Bill C-45. We wanted the council's support to have government start enforcing the *Criminal Code* in relation to the Westray Bill.

The next morning (March 11), the USW group, myself, members of Injured Workers Association, and numerous concerned residents met outside Peter MacKay's office. Unfortunately, we hadn't done our homework and Peter was out of town that day.

The USW group had previously arranged to meet with some officials at Province House in Halifax at noon on the 11th, followed by a lunch break, then additional meetings beginning at 1:30 P.M. Once the meetings were completed, the agenda was for the USW members to fly out of Halifax and return to Toronto.

The twenty-fifth anniversary of the Westray disaster was coming up. Time has a way of passing quickly, yet, during a stressful time, slowing down. I had decided to tell my story so that people could understand how lives are affected by being forced to work in unsafe conditions. Bill C-45 is meant to tell employers and corporate executives that they will be held responsible for their actions and to think twice before forcing employees to work unsafely.

In my opinion education is the key—the more educated, the better informed. I hope my story helps to educate the masses and nobody goes through what I did. I've thrown my pride aside and opened up about my learning disability in hopes that others out there know they're not alone and help is there; all you have to do is ask.

Straight Good News posted my twentieth-anniversary speech on YouTube, May 2012.

January 2017

The twenty-fifth anniversary of Westray was approaching. It was hard to believe that twenty-five years ago my world changed. I am the only one (that I know of) who went from working in the mine to lobbying for (and getting passed) the Westray Bill. This wouldn't have been possible without the strong support and help from the United Steelworkers Union. I was there at the beginning and saw it through to the end.

Early in January I received an email from Del Paré, informing me of her intention to attend the ceremony for the twenty-fifth anniversary in Stellarton. My reply to that first email was to ask if Peter Boyle was attending as well. Her reply was affirmative, and I was looking forward to the reunion of us three. We were part of the team (including the late Dennis Deveaux) that lobbied Parliament three times. We were together constantly for approximately three weeks until the bill finally passed.

The author and Peter Boyle at the Westray memorial.

MARCH 2017

In the middle of March, I contacted Sylvia Boyce. Unofficially, I had heard that the USW wanted to be a part of the ceremony by sending a representative. Sylvia confirmed that something was being planned, but she did not have the details and would get back to me when everything was firmly in place.

APRIL 2017

In the middle of April, I received a communication from Del asking that I retrieve her from the Stanfield International Airport on May 7 at 6:30 A.M. Peter had decided to drive rather than fly. He planned to leave Ontario on May 6 arriving in the late afternoon of May 7.

MAY 7, 2017

Everything was working out like clockwork. I picked up Del at the airport in Halifax, and Peter arrived in Pictou County almost simultaneously. Peter was accompanied by Mike Seaward, retired president of United Steelworkers Local 8412 and vice-president of the Labour Council of Toronto and York region. Although retired, Mike is a popular figure amongst the Steelworkers and still very active in a lot of their various good works.

It had been pre-planned the month before that Del, Peter, and I would meet at the Tara Motel (located in New Glasgow minutes from the Westray site) after Del and I arrived from the airport. We had a late supper at the Thistle Bar & Grill and caught up on each others' lives. It was just a relaxing evening of friends getting together after a long time—talking and watching the hockey playoffs.

As we were leaving the bar we ran into Al Bieksa of the BC Federation of Labour. After Mike made the introduction, I learned that Al's son was a National Hockey League player. Hockey is a sport that is near and dear to my heart and the conversation flowed easily between us. Unbeknownst to me, Al was to be a speaker the next day and that was why he was in town.

May 8, 2017

The twenty-fifth anniversary of the Westray disaster was a huge milestone—events including speakers as well as workshops were planned. The agenda was packed full and I didn't know if I could attend all, but my goal was to attend as many as physically possible. That would mean starting my day at dawn and continuing far into the night for four days straight.

The Museum of Industry was the focal point for the majority of the events. Besides the permanent display on the second floor (for the miners) there was another display on the main floor. On display in the main lobby were pictures of the twenty-six lost miners, a lunch can belonging to Eugene Johnson, a miniature representation of the tunnels, a flag belonging to the Steelworkers, and literature pertaining to Westray. The Steelworkers' flag was significant because it was signed by the various MPs and interested parties after Bill C-45 was given royal assent in 2003.

My day started at 7 A.M. I was out of the house by 9 A.M. and went to the hotel to retrieve Peter, Del, and Mike. We went straight to the museum to hear the opening remarks, and the first of many scheduled speakers. The first break was at 10:45 A.M. so we went out to the main lobby to look at the display. As I was looking at the pictures of the lost miners, I touched Eric McIsaac's photo and said to Del, "This is one of the first miners I worked with underground."

We rejoined the group for lunch, then attended the rest of the afternoon's seminars and workshops. The first day adjourned at 4 P.M. A supper was held at Piper's Landing in Pictou by the Steelworkers for families of Westray. When Del, Peter, and I arrived I noticed that some of the women were being given silver ribbons. When I asked what the significance was of the silver ribbons I was told they were for the widows of the twenty-six lost miners.

The first lady I approached wearing one of the silver ribbons was the widow of Eric McIsaac, whose picture I touched at the museum. I had never met her before and believe it was fate that we met that night. Her daughter informed me that her mother was still having issues with her husband's death and didn't like to speak about that period of time. Upon hearing this, I had a serious discussion with her explaining that talking about it helps to relieve some of the pain.

For me the first day ended around 11:30 P.M.

MAY 9, 2017

Day two I was up at 5:30 A.M. and on the move by 6:00 A.M. Once again I picked up Del, Peter, and Mike at their hotel and we proceeded to Summer Street Industries. Everyone connected with the twenty-fifth-anniversary events was gathering for a march to Westray Memorial Park at 6:45 A.M. On the agenda at the park was a prayer by Reverend Jim Webber-Cook and several short speeches. Afterwards we were returning to Summer Street Industries for light refreshments.

Several of us who attended the walk returned to the Museum of Industry where the seminars and workshops continued throughout the day. The day before, some of the Steelworkers had gone to the local high schools giving speeches about Westray, the passing of Bill C-45, and what workers' rights were in relation to refusing to do unsafe work.

A limited number of students from each school were invited to attend a luncheon at the museum the day of the anniversary. I had the pleasure of seven students at my table. The conversation flowed freely with lots of questions and answers from both sides. My hope is that the students learned something very important that day—safety first.

After lunch, the students returned to their respective schools. Del, Peter, and Mike returned to their hotel, and I decided to go home to see if I could fit in a quick nap before the evening events began. A nap was not to happen—my wife informed me that CBC Radio had called requesting an interview for their early morning show (with Anna Maria Tremonti) to be aired the next morning. When I returned the call I was given the choice of a live interview or pre-recorded. Because it was the day after the twenty-fifth anniversary, and with all the emotions involved, I didn't trust myself to be able to complete the interview so I chose to pre-record. The interview was pre-recorded at 7 A.M. the next morning and aired at 9 A.M.

Steelworkers meet with students to discuss Westray and workplace safety. Clockwise from left: Del Paré (back shown), students Morgan Wilkens, Torri O'Brien, Taya MacLean, Lyndsay MacPherson, the author, Emily Cooley, and Taylor Fraser, and the USW's Lawrence McBrearty.

It rained pretty much all day so I decided to arrive at the memorial service early (it was scheduled for 7 A.M.). With my children and grandchildren in tow, we arrived at the site while it was still light and decided to take some pictures. Meanwhile people were starting to arrive for the service, including the media. Colleen Jones of CBC was on-site and we had a short interview where I displayed my Medal of Bravery (which I always carry to any event concerning Westray) for the camera. [Both interviews are available online.]

Even though it was still raining, the service was held as scheduled, with a reception afterwards at the Museum of Industry. The reception lasted a few hours and I was home around 11:30 P.M. Knowing I had to get up early for the radio interview, I tried to get some rest. I had one more day to go of this getting up early and arriving home late in the evening. After two days this schedule

*Marty Warren, District 6 USW director, was part of the
Steelworkers' group at the twenty-fifth memorial.*

was beginning to take its toll. I was tired and my energy level was
low. I was also an emotional wreck because the memories of those
fateful days were at the forefront of my mind. It was almost, but not
quite, like living them all over again.

MAY 10, 2017

Up early again, waiting for the phone to ring so I could do my phone
interview with CBC. After that was completed I lay down for a short
nap before going to get Del, Peter, and Mike for the final day of the
anniversary events. We met at the hotel at 10:00 A.M. and headed

The author and his co-writer, Marjorie Coady, pose for a photo while at work on this book in New Glasgow.

over to the museum. We sat in on a health and safety workshop until lunch. After lunch, we decided to tour the various mining interests (including the Westray site) in Pictou County.

This tour took up most of the afternoon. While at the museum earlier, a group (us included) arranged with Debbie and Allen Martin to have a farewell dinner at their home in Fox Brook. It was meant to be a relaxing evening to help everyone wind down from the hectic schedule that the last four days had incurred. The evening was a success. Everyone left Debbie and Allen's home full and in good spirits.

2017

Marjorie Coady and I finished writing this book, which we hope will ensure that the lessons of Westray are not lost. **No More Westrays**.

TIMELINE

SEPTEMBER II, 1991   Westray mine opens in Plymouth, NS.

DECEMBER 1991   The author starts work at the Westray mine.

MAY 9, 1992   The mine explodes, killing twenty-six men.

MAY 9, 1992   Off-shift at the time of the explosion, the author volunteers as a barefaced rescuer.

MAY 13, 1992   The rescue ends with fifteen bodies recovered.

MAY 15, 1992   Justice K. Peter Richard is appointed to head an inquiry into the disaster.

APRIL 1993   RCMP announce charges of manslaughter and criminal negligence causing death against Curragh Resources Inc. and mine managers Gerald Phillips and Roger Parry.

NOVEMBER 1994   The author receives the Medal of Bravery for his part in the Westray rescue effort.

1997   The author is officially diagnosed with PTSD.

DECEMBER 1997   The province says it will accept all seventy-four recommendations of the Westray Report.

JUNE 30, 1998   The Public Prosecution Service announces that the criminal prosecution against Phillips, Parry, and Curragh has ended.

OCTOBER 24, 1999 · The author makes his first trip to Ottawa.

NOVEMBER 7, 2003 · After years of lobbying by families and the Steelworkers, the Westray Bill (now Bill C-54) becomes law.

MAY 9, 2012 · Twentieth anniversary at Westray memorial in Pictou County.

SEPTEMBER 2015 · The first charge is laid in Nova Scotia under the Westray law. The owner of an auto shop in Dartmouth is charged after a mechanic dies while working under a car.

MAY 9, 2017 · The author attends twenty-fifth-anniversary memorial and meets with local students as part of the Steelworkers' ongoing safety education campaign.

ACKNOWLEDGEMENTS

MY HEARTFELT APPRECIATION GOES OUT TO THE UNITED Steelworkers (formerly the United Steelworkers of America) for their invaluable assistance. Especially Peter Boyle who provided some of the photos featured inside as well as his memories of dates, times, and the politics of the lobbying. Also Sylvia Boyce, Lawrence McBrearty and Ken Neumann who supplied me with support and information during the book-writing process.

The twenty-six miners we lost on that fateful day were my inspiration for wanting this book to be printed. My hope is that their ultimate sacrifice is not in vain.

I would also like to thank Nimbus Publishing—namely Elaine McCluskey (editor)—for patiently guiding me through the publishing/editing process.

It goes without saying that my wife and children are greatly appreciated because they lived through this journey with me.

And last but not least my sister Nancy who transcribed my original notes onto paper. Also my cousin Marjorie Coady for putting into words this incredible journey that is still continuing.

PHOTO CREDITS

All photos are supplied by the author with the exception of:

Nova Scotia Museum of Industry: p. 25, p. 136 (four photos);
Insert (two photos: ballcap and bolter)

The Canadian Press: p. 42, p. 48